The Ultimate Clean Eating Cookbook

1000 Days Healthy Recipes and 4-Week Meal Plans to Help You Living Health

Janet Douglas

Contents

Introduction 5
Key Principles of Clean Eating 6
Health Benefit of Clean Eating 7

Breakfast Recipes 9
Loaded Veggie Avocado Quinoa Frittatas .. 9
Delicious Immune Boosting Wellness Smoothie 10
Blueberry Quinoa Pancakes 11
Banana Spinach Muffins 12
Pineapple Mango Smoothie 13
Breakfast Burritos 14
Whole Wheat Coconut Banana Waffles 15
Fluffy Whole Wheat Zucchini Bread Pancakes 16

Poultry Recipes 17
Crispy Lemon Rosemary Brick Chicken 17
Balsamic Chicken with Lemony Beans and Mushrooms 18
Almond-Crusted Chicken 19
Chicken Meatballs and Cauliflower Rice 20
Lemon and Basil Chicken Breasts 22
Chicken Breasts Stuffed with Goat Cheese 23
Lemon Chicken with Sautéed Squash 24
Chicken Cutlets with White Wine Butter Sauce 25
Sticky Honey Garlic Chicken Wings 26

Pesto Pasta with Ground Turkey 27
Spicy Ground Turkey Stir-Fried with Green Bean 28
Chicken Fried Rice with Pineapple 29
Beef-Stuffed Peppers 31
Korean Beef 32
Healthy Beef and Broccoli 33
Moroccan Lamb Tagine 34
Grilled Flank Steak with Mustardy Potato Salad 35
Taco-Stuffed Zucchini 36
Meatball Spaghetti Squash Boats 37
Garlic Lime Flank Steak 38
Ground Beef and Sweet Potato Chili 39
Instant Pot Beef Stew Recipe 40

Pork Recipes 41
Garlic Lime Pork Chops 41
Herb Crusted Pork Chops 42
Honey Chipotle Pork Roast 43
Quinoa Fried Rice with Pork 44
One Pan Roasted Pork Tenderloin with Veggies 45
Pork Chops with Balsamic Peppers 46

Seafood Recipes 47
Teriyaki Salmon Recipe 47
Tuna Burgers 48

Spicy Orange Shrimp Recipe 49

Walnut Crusted Cod 50

Popcorn Shrimp 51

Brazilian Fish Stew 52

Lemon Garlic Baked Salmon with Asparagus 54

Tuna Stuffed Avocado 55

Pan Seared Salmon with Chia Seeds 56

Coconut Lemongrass Scallops with Lime .. 57

Salmon Chowder 58

Dijon Salmon with Green Bean Pilaf 59

Soups and Salad 60

Broccoli Cheese Soup 60

Curried Coconut Pumpkin Soup 61

Asparagus Soup 62

Chicken Pot Pie Soup 63

Sweet Potato and Arugula Salad 64

Kale Apple and Quinoa Salad 65

Strawberry Spinach Salad with Chicken and Avocado 66

Cucumber Salad 67

Snack and Side Recipes 68

Grain Free Rosemary Crackers 68

Tuna Pinwheels 69

Doritos 70

Roasted Curried Chickpeas 71

Baked Garlic Parmesan Potato Wedges ... 72

Garlic Butter Quinoa 73

Easy Roasted Baby Bok Choy 74

Deviled Eggs 75

Vegetarian Recipes 76

Lentils and Rice 76

Chickpea Tacos 77

Butternut Squash Risotto 78

Sweet Potato Curry 79

Sautéed Zucchini with Mint, Basil & Pine Nuts 80

Red Cabbage Pasta 81

Chickpea Basil Quinoa Salad 82

Corn Casserole 83

Lentil Sloppy Joes 84

Dessert Recipes 85

Carrot Cake 85

Peach & Blueberry Cobbler 86

Strawberry Nice Cream 87

Mango Fruit Leather 88

Dark Chocolate Frozen Banana Bites 89

Greek Yogurt with Warm Berry Sauce 90

Tropical Fruit Pudding 91

4 Weeks Meal Plan 92

1st Week Meal Plan 92

2nd Week Meal Plan 93

3rd Week Meal Plan 94

4th Week Meal Plan 95

Conclusion 96

Introduction

Clean Eating is essentially a diet, just a way of eating. But it is also a lifestyle that is great for improving health and well-being.

Clean Eating is traditionally defined as simple, healthy eating without artificial ingredients. This typically involves eliminating most processed foods, trans fats, heavy saturated fats, added sugars, and refined grains. And some are opting for a healthy diet by also eliminating gluten, dairy and soy.

For those looking to improve their diet, learning about healthy eating can be a great place to start. Especially when the value is placed on whole and nutritious foods such as fruits, vegetables, whole grain products and high quality protein, as they make up the majority of a balanced diet. But it's also important to note that just because a food isn't considered "clean" doesn't automatically mean "dirty" or bad for you.

Some research also suggests that the quality of your food choices can be important for weight loss. However, eating less processed foods doesn't compensate for the need to control calories in the first place.

Key Principles of Clean Eating

1. Pick Whole Foods

The basic idea of healthy eating is to choose foods that are as close as possible to their natural form. So instead of boxed, bagged or packed foods, choose fresh, whole foods. Think of a whole turkey instead of frozen turkey meatballs or raw grapes instead of rubbery sandwiches with juice. Bonus: if you avoid highly processed foods like chips, cookies, and convenience foods, you are skipping their calories, sugar, salt, and saturated fat.

2. Eat More Whole Grains

Refined carbohydrates like white bread, pasta, and rice lose nutrients during the manufacturing process. Swap them for whole grain bread and pasta and brown or wild rice. Or opt for other whole grain products such as oatmeal, popcorn, barley or bulgur. This change can have a big impact: studies show that a diet high in whole grains can lower your risk of heart disease, type 2 diabetes, and colon cancer.

3. Eat Fruits and Vegetables

These natural foods are two staple foods for a healthy diet. Some clean eaters say that all of their produce should be fresh. However, others say that frozen and canned options are the better option because they contain the same amount of nutrients. Just read the label to make sure you haven't added any sugar or salt. Also, choose whole fruits rather than juices, which contain less fibre and more sugar. Aim to eat at least five to nine servings of fruits and vegetables per day, depending on your calorie needs and your physical activity.

4. Watch Out for Salt and Added Sugar

Clean foods are inherently low in salt and sugar, and adding them goes against the most natural approach possible. Since processed foods are a major source, you can reduce your intake by avoiding them. Otherwise, read food labels for added sweeteners and salt, even in foods that look healthy, like yogurt or ketchup. Also watch how much you add to your food and drinks. Instead, try seasoning with spices and herbs.

5. Skip the Artificial Ingredients

Artificial colors, sweeteners, preservatives and other ingredients have no place in a healthy diet. Read food labels at the supermarket and avoid items that contain counterfeit products.

Health Benefit of Clean Eating

1. More Energy

Eating a healthy diet that properly nourishes your body will help you feel more energetic and productive. Several nutrients, including B vitamins and iron, help cells access fuel so they can function properly.

Eating a healthy diet will also help regulate your blood sugar and help you avoid fatigue-inducing blood sugar spikes that can occur after consuming processed carbohydrates like sweets or refined grains. Michigan State University Extension recommends increasing your energy level with a breakfast that contains whole grains high in fibre which provides energy until lunch.

2. Better Mental Health

Healthy eating not only promotes your physical well-being, but also your mental health. Some of the nutrients in your diet, like vitamin B-6, help produce dopamine, a chemical involved in pleasure.

Omega-3 fatty acids also promote good mental health, while a deficiency can lead to bad mood and depression. Limiting caffeine can also improve mental health (it can increase anxiety), and not skipping meals can help prevent stress or abdominal pain.

3. Cancer Prevention

Eat a healthy diet and this will also help fight the growth of cancer. A diet high in processed foods increases your risk of cancer, according to the Colorado State University Extension, and saturated fat, processed meat, and fried foods increase your risk of cancer.

On the flip side, eating a healthy diet rich in fruits and vegetables increases your intake of phytonutrients and antioxidants that fight cancer growth. The state of Colorado promotes cruciferous vegetables, a family that includes broccoli and kale, and tomatoes, as particularly useful.

4. Improved Cardiovascular Health

Clean Eating promotes long-term health because eating a healthy diet helps reduce the risk of cardiovascular disease. For example, fruits and vegetables contain vitamin C, a nutrient that helps maintain the strength of blood vessels. A diet rich in fruits and vegetables reduces the risk of coronary heart disease and also protects against stroke and high blood pressure.

Eating a healthy diet high in healthy fats, such as those found in nuts, avocados, and olive oil, lowers harmful cholesterol levels, which also fights cardiovascular disease. On the other hand, an unhealthy diet high in saturated fat will raise your blood cholesterol levels, which will put your cardiovascular health at risk.

5. Weight Loss

Most people lose weight when they eat a healthy diet. Eating mostly whole foods means you are consuming fewer nutritious calories, even though you are eating more food more often. Plus, a diet complete with vitamins, minerals, phytochemicals, and antioxidants helps alleviate cravings, speeds up sluggish metabolism, and lets you lose weight without feeling hungry or starved.

Many obesity-related health problems can even be reversibly prevented by eating healthy, healthy and natural foods. This is because you get more nutrients from your food, but also because when you consume processed and packaged foods, you consume preservatives, artificial sweeteners, sugar, packaging chemicals, and pesticides.

A healthy and complete diet has many benefits. Processed and packaged foods contain dangerous toxins, sugars, preservatives, and a host of other harmful ingredients that lead to obesity, health problems, lack of energy, and a weakened immune system. Improve your health, weight and happiness by eating healthy.

Breakfast Recipes

Loaded Veggie Avocado Quinoa Frittatas

Ingredients:

- 1 cup uncooked quinoa
- 6 large eggs
- 1 cup spinach, chopped
- 2 tablespoons chopped cilantro
- 1 small red bell pepper, diced
- ¼ cup diced red onion
- 1 ripe avocado, diced
- ¼ teaspoon salt
- freshly cracked black pepper

Prep Time:	15 minutes
Cook Time:	25 minutes
Serves:	12

Preparation:

1. In a small pot over high heat, combine the quinoa and 2 cups of water. Bring to a boil, cover, and simmer for 15 minutes, or until all of the water has been absorbed. Transfer to a separate bowl to cool for 10 to 15 minutes after fluffing with a fork.
2. Preheat the oven to 350°F. Spray the interior of each muffin liner with non-stick cooking spray and line a 12-cup muffin tray with muffin liners.
3. In a large mixing bowl, whisk together the eggs. Combine the vegetables, onion, avocado, salt and pepper, and jalapeno and/or cheese in a mixing bowl (if adding). Fold in the quinoa that has been let to chill.
4. Divide evenly between the muffin tins. Bake for 20 to 25 minutes, or until the egg has set and the edges are just beginning to become golden brown.
5. Allow it cool for 5 to 10 minutes in the pan.

Serving Suggestion: Serve the Loaded Veggie Avocado Quinoa Frittatas with dipping sauce.

Variation Tip: Use millet.

Nutritional Information Per Serving:

Calories 113| Fat 5g |Sodium 5mg | Carbs 49.3g | Fibre 2.2g | Sugar 1g | Protein 4.7g

Delicious Immune Boosting Wellness Smoothie

Ingredients:
- 1 frozen ripe banana
- 1 cup frozen pineapple
- 2 to 3 cups organic spinach
- 1 knob fresh ginger, peeled
- 1 knob turmeric root, peeled
- ½ tablespoon honey
- ⅛ teaspoon freshly ground black pepper
- ½ to ¾ cup coconut milk

Prep Time:	05 minutes
Cook Time:	00 minutes
Serves:	1

Preparation:

Combine all ingredients in a large high-powered blender and blend on high for 1 to 2 minutes, or until well incorporated. If the smoothie is too thick, add more almond milk. This recipe makes one smoothie.

Serving Suggestion: Serve the Delicious Immune Boosting Wellness Smoothie with chips.

Variation Tip: Use Maple syrup.

Nutritional Information Per Serving:

Calories 253| Fat 3g |Sodium 5mg | Carbs 60.3g | Fibre 7.6g | Sugar 0.6g | Protein 7g

Blueberry Quinoa Pancakes

Ingredients:

Dry Ingredients

- 1 cup quinoa, cooked and cooled
- ¾ cup all-purpose flour or whole wheat pastry flour
- 2 teaspoons baking powder
- ¼ teaspoon salt

Wet Ingredients

- 1 large egg
- ⅓ cup fresh lemon juice
- zest of 1 large lemon
- ¼ cup unsweetened coconut milk
- 2 tablespoons coconut sugar
- 1 teaspoon pure vanilla extract
- 1 tablespoon olive oil
- ¾ cup fresh or frozen blueberries

Prep Time:	20 minutes
Cook Time:	15 minutes
Serves:	2

Preparation:

1. In a medium-sized bowl, mix the cooked and cooled quinoa, flour, baking powder and salt.
2. In another medium bowl, stir together the egg, lemon juice and zest, milk, honey, vanilla (or almond extract) and olive oil until smooth.
3. Add the wet ingredients to the dry ingredients and whisk, then carefully fold in the blueberries. If the batter is too thick, add a dash of milk.
4. Lightly coat a large non-stick pan or grill pan with olive oil and set over medium heat. Pour ¼ cup of batter into the pan. Cook until bubbles appear on top, about 2 minutes. Turn the cakes over and bake for 2 minutes, until golden brown on the underside. Clean the pan and repeat the process with more melted butter and the remaining batter. You may need to turn the heat down to medium after the second round to avoid burning.
5. Top with fresh fruit, little honey, nut butter or maple syrup.

Serving Suggestion: Serve the Blueberry Quinoa Pancakes with maple syrup.

Variation Tip: Use almond milk in case not having coconut milk.

Nutritional Information Per Serving:

Calories 281| Fat 5.2g |Sodium 5mg | Carbs 49.3g | Fibre 7.6g | Sugar 9.6g | Protein 7.1g

Banana Spinach Muffins

Ingredients:

- 2 eggs
- 2 medium-to-large extra ripe bananas
- ¼ cup pure maple syrup
- ⅓ cup coconut free milk
- 3 cups spinach
- 1 teaspoon vanilla extract
- 1 cup packed blanched almond flour
- 1 cup oat flour, gluten-free if desired
- ¼ cup flaxseed meal
- 1 teaspoon cinnamon
- 1 teaspoon baking powder
- ½ teaspoon baking soda
- ¼ teaspoon salt

Prep Time:	10 minutes
Cook Time:	20 to 25 minutes
Serves:	10

Preparation:

1. Preheat oven to 375°F. Using 10 muffin liners (we're just making 10 muffins), line a muffin tray. To prevent the muffins from sticking to the liners, spray the insides with non-stick cooking spray.
2. In a large, high-powered blender, combine the eggs, bananas, maple syrup, coconut milk, spinach, and vanilla extract. Blend on high for 1 minute, or until totally smooth. Remove from the equation.
3. Whisk together the almond flour, oat flour, flaxseed meal, cinnamon, baking powder, baking soda, and salt in a large mixing basin until thoroughly blended. Pour the mixed wet components over the dry ingredients and stir until fully integrated with a wooden spoon. If you're using hemp hearts, feel free to stir them in. Divide the batter between the muffin liners. Bake for 20 to 25 minutes or until a toothpick comes out clean or with just a few crumbs attached.

Serving Suggestion: Serve the Banana Spinach Muffins with honey.

Variation Tip: Use kale or your choice of greens in case not having spinach.

Nutritional Information Per Serving:

Calories 177| Fat 8.2g |Sodium 5mg | Carbs 22.3g | Fibre 3.6g | Sugar 7.6g | Protein 6g

Pineapple Mango Smoothie

Ingredients:

- 1 cup frozen mango chunks
- ¾ cup frozen pineapple chunks
- 1¼ cups light almond milk, plus more as necessary

Preparation:

Combine all ingredients in a large high-powered blender and blend on high for 1 to 2 minutes, or until well incorporated. If the smoothie is too thick, add more almond milk. This recipe makes one smoothie.

Serving Suggestion: Serve the Pineapple Mango Smoothie with cookies.

Variation Tip: Use coconut milk in case not having almond milk.

Nutritional Information Per Serving:

Calories 336| Fat 17.2g |Sodium 5mg | Carbs 39.3g | Fibre 3.6g | Sugar 25.6g | Protein 1.7g

Prep Time:	05 minutes
Cook Time:	00 minutes
Serves:	1

Breakfast Burritos

Ingredients:

- 6 (8-inch) whole wheat tortillas
- 3 medium-sweet potatoes
- 1 (15-ounce) can black beans, rinsed and drained
- ½ teaspoon cumin
- ¼ teaspoon chili powder
- few dashes of red pepper flakes, if desired
- 6 large eggs
- 1 avocado, diced
- ½ cup shredded Mexican cheese
- ⅓ cup red enchilada sauce

Prep Time:	20 minutes
Cook Time:	05 minutes
Serves:	6

Preparation:

1. Cooking the sweet potatoes: Prick the sweet potatoes several times with a fork. Microwave and microwave on high power for 4 to 6 minutes or until cooked through. It can take up to 10 minutes depending on the thickness of the sweet potatoes. Alternatively, you can roast them in the oven at 375°F for 45 minutes or until tender. Once the sweet potatoes are cooked, remove the skin and place the potatoes in a medium bowl. Mix with a fork and put aside.
2. In a separate large bowl, add black beans, cumin, chili powder and red pepper flakes, if desired. Stir to combine, then set aside.
3. In a separate medium bowl, beat the eggs (or egg whites). Spray a pan with non-stick cooking spray and set over medium-low heat. Add the eggs and cook. Fold every few minutes to make fluffy eggs. Remove from heat after cooking.
4. To make burritos, make sure you have lightly warmed tortillas; makes them easier to roll. You can microwave them for 10 to 20 seconds before putting them together. Place the hot tortillas on top and evenly distribute the mashed sweet potatoes on top, as shown in the video. Spread the scrambled eggs, diced avocado, black beans and grated cheese evenly over each tortilla. Then pour a tablespoon of enchilada sauce over each one. Season with salt and pepper, if desired. Tuck in the ends and roll the burritos.
5. Reheat: Place on a baking sheet in the oven at 300°F for 5 to 10 minutes or simply in the microwave for a minute or two. Serve with sour cream, Greek yogurt, salsa or hot sauce.

Serving Suggestion: Serve the Breakfast Burritos with dipping sauce.

Variation Tip: Use potatoes in case not having sweet potato.

Nutritional Information Per Serving:

Calories 395| Fat 13.2g |Sodium 5mg | Carbs 54.3g | Fibre 12.6g | Sugar 5.6g | Protein 17g

Whole Wheat Coconut Banana Waffles

Ingredients:

- ⅔ cup unsalted raw almonds
- 1¼ cups whole wheat flour
- 2 teaspoons baking powder
- 1 teaspoon baking soda
- ½ teaspoon sea salt
- 2 eggs
- 1 egg white
- 2 cups unsweetened almond milk
- 2 teaspoons fresh lemon juice
- ¼ cup coconut oil
- 1 large ripe banana
- ⅓ cup unsweetened coconut flakes
- 3 ounces dark chocolate, chopped

Prep Time:	05 minutes
Cook Time:	20 minutes
Serves:	8

Preparation:

1. Preheat the oven to 350°F.
2. Place the almonds on a baking sheet and divide them. Bake for about 8 minutes. Remove and let cool on a baking sheet for 5 minutes. Reduce oven temperature to 300 °F.
3. Place the almonds in a food processor and mix until finely ground. Transfer to a large bowl and add the flour, baking powder, baking soda and salt.
4. In a medium bowl, whisk together the eggs, egg white, almond milk, lemon juice and coconut oil. Mix the wet ingredients with the dry ingredients, then add the mashed banana and coconut flakes.
5. Spray the waffle iron with cooking oil. Pour about 1 cup of batter evenly over the griddle. The amount of batter you need will depend on your waffle iron, so use common sense here. Bake until waffle is golden, about 3 to 4 minutes. Transfer to a baking dish or baking sheet and place in the oven to keep warm while you bake the rest of the waffles.

Serving Suggestion: Serve the Whole Wheat Coconut Banana Waffles with yogurt or berries.

Variation Tip: Use almond flour in case not having whole wheat flour.

Nutritional Information Per Serving:

Calories 281| Fat 16.2g |Sodium 5mg | Carbs 29.3g | Fibre 3.6g | Sugar 6g | Protein 6.8g

Fluffy Whole Wheat Zucchini Bread Pancakes

Ingredients:

Dry Ingredients:

- 1 cup whole wheat pastry flour or white whole wheat flour
- 2 teaspoons baking powder
- 1¼ teaspoons cinnamon
- ¼ teaspoon nutmeg
- ¼ teaspoon salt

Wet Ingredients:

- 1 heaping cup shredded zucchini, squeezed of excess moisture with a paper towel
- 1 egg
- 2 tablespoons pure maple syrup
- 1 tablespoon melted and cooled coconut oil
- 1 teaspoon vanilla extract
- ½ cup unsweetened vanilla almond milk
- ¼ cup chopped pecans, optional

Prep Time:	10 minutes
Cook Time:	10 minutes
Serves:	4

Preparation:

1. In a large bowl, whisk together the whole puff pastry, baking powder, cinnamon, nutmeg and salt.
2. In a separate large bowl, combine the grated zucchini, egg, maple syrup, coconut oil, vanilla and almond milk until smooth and blended. Stir in nuts if used.
3. Add the dry ingredients to the wet ingredients and mix until they barely combine. If the dough seems too thick, add a little more milk. If it is very wet, add another tablespoon of flour.
4. Lightly brush a large non-stick skillet or grill pan with coconut oil or butter and heat over medium heat. Put the dough into mold to ⅓-full and spread it a little with a spoon if necessary. Cook until bubbles appear on top, about 2 minutes.
5. Flip the cakes and bake for 2 minutes until golden brown. Clean the pan and repeat the process with more coconut oil (or butter) and the rest of the batter. You may need to lower the heat after the second batch to avoid burns.

Serving Suggestion: Serve the Fluffy Whole Wheat Zucchini Bread Pancakes with maple syrup.

Variation Tip: Use coconut flour in case not having whole wheat flour.

Nutritional Information Per Serving:

Calories 200| Fat 5.2g |Sodium 5.3mg | Carbs 32.3g | Fibre 5.6g | Sugar 7.6g | Protein 5g

Poultry Recipes

Crispy Lemon Rosemary Brick Chicken

Ingredients:

- 2 tablespoons chopped fresh rosemary
- 3 cloves garlic, chopped
- 1 lemon, zested
- ¾ teaspoon each sea salt and ground black pepper, divided
- 1 tablespoon Dijon mustard
- 1 tablespoon olive oil
- 4 (8-ounce) bone-in and skin-on chicken breasts

Preparation:

1. Preheat a greased grill over medium-to-high heat with half the grill turned off to create a cool zone.
2. Place the rosemary, garlic, lemon zest and ⅔ of the salt and pepper on a board and finely chop until a sticky paste forms. Place in a small bowl. Add mustard and oil.
3. Gently slide your fingers under the skin of the chicken and rub the herb mixture underneath. Season the chicken on both sides with the remaining ⅓ of the salt and pepper. (Make Ahead: Prepare chicken up to 2 days ahead. Cover and refrigerate. Let stand at room temperature for 30 minutes before grilling).
4. Place the chicken skin side down on the hot side of the grill. Place a brick wrapped in foil on each chicken breast and cover the grill. If you are using cast iron pans, place a piece of foil on each chicken breast, then place the pans on top.
5. Cook until the skin is golden and crisp, about 10 minutes, then move the chicken to a cool place.
6. If there are germs or the chicken starts to burn. Remove the bricks (or pots and pans) with oven mitts, flip the chicken with tongs, and put the bricks (or pots and pans) back on top.
7. Broil, covered, until an instant thermometer inserted into the thickest part of the larger breast reads 165°F, an additional 8 to 10 minutes. Gently place the chicken skin side up on a plate and let stand 5 minutes before serving.

Prep Time:	10 minutes
Cook Time:	30 minutes
Serves:	4

Serving Suggestion: Serve the Crispy Lemon Rosemary Brick Chicken with salad.

Variation Tip: Use turkey breast in case not having chicken breast.

Nutritional Information Per Serving:

Calories 301| Fat 12g |Sodium 543mg | Carbs 2g | Fibre 0g | Sugar 0g | Protein 40g

Balsamic Chicken with Lemony Beans and Mushrooms

Ingredients:

- 1 pound green beans, trimmed and rinsed
- 2 teaspoons olive oil, divided
- 1 pound button mushrooms, sliced
- 4 cloves garlic, thinly sliced
- 1 lemon, zested and juiced
- 1 yellow onion, cut into ¼-inch-thick rings
- 1 pound boneless, skinless chicken breast, sliced to ½-inch-thick
- 2 tablespoons balsamic vinegar
- 2 teaspoons dried thyme
- ½ teaspoon sea salt

Preparation:

1. Half fill a large pot with water and bring to a boil. Prepare an ice bath nearby. Add the beans to the pot and reduce the heat to medium to high. Cook until crisp and tender, about 5 minutes. Drain and immerse in an ice bath. Drain again and set aside.
2. In a large non-stick skillet, heat 1 teaspoon of oil over medium heat. Add the mushrooms and cook for 8 to 10 minutes, stirring occasionally. Add the garlic, lemon zest and juice and sauté for 1 minute. Add the beans and heat. Remove from heat and cover to keep warm.
3. Meanwhile, in a separate large non-stick skillet, heat the remaining 1 teaspoon of oil over medium heat. Add the onion and sauté for 5 minutes. Add the chicken, vinegar, thyme and salt and cook, stirring frequently for 8 minutes, until the chicken is cooked through. Remove the stove. Divide the chicken and bean mixes between plates and drizzle the chicken with the cooking juices.

Prep Time:	35 minutes
Cook Time:	35 minutes
Serves:	4

Serving Suggestion: Serve the Balsamic Chicken with Lemony Beans and Mushrooms with salad.

Variation Tip: Use turkey breast in case not having chicken breast.

Nutritional Information Per Serving:

Calories 235| Fat 4g |Sodium 332mg | Carbs 19g | Fibre 6g | Sugar 8g | Protein 31g

Almond-Crusted Chicken

Ingredients:

Sauce

- 1 cup chopped seeded Roma tomatoes
- 1 cup jarred roasted red peppers, drained
- ¼ cup low-sodium chicken broth
- 2 teaspoons olive oil
- 1 clove garlic, minced
- 1 tablespoon fresh lemon juice

Chicken

- ½ cup whole-grain baguette cubes
- ¼ cup sliced unsalted almonds
- 2 tablespoons whole-wheat flour
- 2 tablespoons grated Parmesan cheese
- ¼ teaspoon each sea salt and ground black pepper
- ¼ cup low-sodium chicken broth
- 8 chicken tenders (about 1 pound)
- 1 tablespoon olive oil

Prep Time:	20 minutes
Cook Time:	20 minutes
Serves:	4

Preparation:

1. Prepare the sauce: Combine the tomatoes, red peppers and ¼ cup of the broth in a food processor until smooth. Heat 2 teaspoons of oil in a small saucepan over medium heat. Add the garlic and cook, stirring frequently, until fragrant about 30 seconds. Add the tomato mixture and cook, stirring occasionally, until slightly thickened for 5 to 7 minutes. Add the lemon juice and stir. Remove from heat and cover to keep warm.
2. Clean the food processor. Add the baguette and work into coarse crumbs. Add the almonds and pulse until coarsely chopped. Transfer to a shallow bowl. In a second flat plate, combine the flour, cheese, salt and pepper. Pour ¼ cup of broth into a third shallow bowl.
3. Line a baking sheet with parchment paper. Dredge the chicken into the flour mixture. Then dip in the broth then in the breadcrumbs and press firmly. Place the chicken on the prepared dish. Discard the rest of the flour, broth and breadcrumbs.
4. In a large skillet, heat 1 tablespoon of oil over medium heat. Add the chicken and cook, turning once, until golden brown and no longer pink inside, 4 to 5 minutes per side. Serve hot with the sauce on zucchini linguine with lemon and oregano.

Serving Suggestion: Serve the Almond-Crusted Chicken with sauce.

Variation Tip: Use walnuts or pecans in case not having almond.

Nutritional Information Per Serving:

Calories 273| Fat 12g |Sodium 5mg | Carbs 13g | Fibre 4g | Sugar 2g | Protein 28g

Chicken Meatballs and Cauliflower Rice

Ingredients:

Meatballs

- non-stick spray
- 1 tablespoon extra-virgin olive oil
- ½ red onion
- 2 garlic cloves, minced
- 1 pound ground chicken
- ¼ cup chopped fresh parsley
- 1 tablespoon Dijon mustard
- ¾ teaspoon kosher salt
- ½ teaspoon freshly ground black pepper

Sauce

- one 14-ounce can coconut milk
- 1¼ cups chopped fresh parsley, divided
- 4 scallions, roughly chopped
- 1 garlic clove, peeled and smashed
- zest and juice of 1 lemon
- kosher salt and freshly ground black pepper
- red pepper flakes, for serving

Cauliflower Rice

- 1 head cauliflower
- 1 to 2 tablespoons olive oil
- salt and freshly ground black pepper, to taste

Prep Time:	05 minutes
Cook Time:	25 minutes
Serves:	4

Preparation:

1. **Make the Balls:** Preheat the oven to 375°F. Line a baking sheet with foil and spray with non-stick spray.
2. In a medium skillet, heat olive oil over medium heat. Add onion and sauté until tender, about 5 minutes. Add the garlic and sauté for about 1 minute until fragrant.
3. Transfer the onion and garlic to a medium bowl and let cool slightly. Add the chicken, parsley and mustard. Season with salt and pepper. Shape the mixture into 2 tablespoons large balls and place them on a baking sheet.
4. Cook meatballs for 17 to 20 minutes, until firm and cooked through.
5. **Prepare the sauce:** In the bowl of a food processor, combine the coconut milk, parsley, chives, garlic, lemon zest and juice and stir until smooth. Season with salt and pepper.
6. Garnish the balls with paprika flakes and the remaining parsley. Serve over cauliflower rice with the sauce.

Serving Suggestion: Serve the Chicken Meatballs and Cauliflower Rice with soup.

Variation Tip: Use brown rive in case not having cauliflower rice.

Nutritional Information Per Serving:

Calories 205| Fat 13g |Sodium 5mg | Carbs 18g | Fibre 3.6g | Sugar 6g | Protein 20g

Lemon and Basil Chicken Breasts

Ingredients:

- 2 boneless, skinless chicken breasts, trimmed of any fat
- juice and zest of one lemon
- 3 tablespoons of fresh basil, chopped (divided)
- 2 cloves of garlic, minced
- 2 tablespoons olive oil (divided)

Preparation:

1. Place the trimmed chicken breast in a large zippered pocket. Mash chicken breasts with a hammer until ½-inch-thick. Add 1 tablespoon of olive oil, lemon zest, lemon juice, 2½ tablespoons of fresh basil, salt, pepper and chopped garlic. Mix well and marinate in the refrigerator for 1 to 2 hours.
2. Take the chicken out of the refrigerator 10 minutes before cooking. Heat 1 tablespoon of olive oil in a large skillet or skillet over medium heat. Once hot, add the chicken breasts and cook for 4 minutes, then turn them over. Cook another 3 to 4 minutes or until juices run clear. Remove from the heat and let the meat rest for at least 5 minutes before serving. Garnish with the last half tablespoon of fresh basil and additional lemon. Enjoy.

Prep Time:	05 minutes
Cook Time:	20 minutes
Serves:	8

Serving Suggestion: Serve the Lemon and Basil Chicken Breasts with sauce.

Variation Tip: Use turkey breast in case not having chicken breasts.

Nutritional Information Per Serving:

Calories 281| Fat 16.2g |Sodium 5mg | Carbs 29.3g | Fibre 3.6g | Sugar 6g | Protein 16.8g

Chicken Breasts Stuffed with Goat Cheese

Ingredients:

- 5 ounces fresh goat cheese
- 2 tablespoons milk
- 2 cloves garlic, minced
- ⅔ cup chopped fresh arugula
- 1 tablespoon grated lemon zest
- a pinch crushed red pepper flakes
- kosher salt and freshly ground black pepper, to taste
- 6 6-ounce boneless, skinless chicken breast halves
- 2 tablespoons extra-virgin olive oil
- 1 cup dry white wine, such as Sauvignon Blanc
- 1 cup low-sodium chicken stock

Prep Time:	20 minutes
Cook Time:	15 minutes
Serves:	6

Preparation:

1. In a small bowl, combine goat cheese and milk until smooth. Add the garlic, arugula, lemon zest and red pepper flakes. Season to taste with salt and pepper.
2. On the thicker side of each chicken breast, cut out a pocket 3 inches deep. (Be careful not to cut the other side of the breast.) Use your fingers to put the goat cheese mixture in each pocket. Press down on the meat and secure it with a toothpick if necessary.
3. In a large skillet, heat the oil over medium heat. Prepare a lid that is too small for the pan but covers the breasts. Cook the chicken (portioned if necessary) until browned on one side without the lid, 4 to 5 minutes. Flip the breasts, season with salt and pepper and place the small lid on the chicken in the pan. Continue cooking until the chicken is cooked through, another 4 to 5 minutes.
4. Transfer the chicken to a dish. Pour the wine into the pan and scrape off the tasty brown pieces that are stuck to the bottom of the pan. Cook, 1 to 2 minutes over medium heat, until the wine is reduced by about half. Add the chicken broth, season with salt and pepper, and cook until the sauce is reduced to a light syrup, 2 to 3 minutes. Pour the reduction over the chicken and serve.

Serving Suggestion: Serve the Chicken Breasts Stuffed with Goat Cheese with mayo.

Variation Tip: Use any cheese in case not having goat cheese.

Nutritional Information Per Serving:

Calories 335| Fat 12g |Sodium 235mg | Carbs 2g | Fibre 0.6g | Sugar 6g | Protein 48g

Lemon Chicken with Sautéed Squash

Ingredients:

- ⅓ cup plus 2 tablespoons chopped fresh rosemary, divided
- 3 tablespoons dried fennel seeds
- 2 teaspoons ground black pepper, divided
- 5 cloves garlic, minced
- ¼ cup fresh lemon juice
- 2 tablespoons reduced-sodium soy sauce
- 6 teaspoons extra-virgin olive oil, divided
- 8-pound whole chicken, rinsed and patted dry
- 3 small sweet potatoes, scrubbed and chopped to ¼-inch pieces
- 1 yellow onion, chopped to ¼-inch pieces
- 2 small zucchinis, chopped to ¼-inch pieces
- 2 small yellow squashes, chopped to ¼-inch pieces

Prep Time:	40 minutes
Cook Time:	2 minutes
Serves:	8

Preparation:

1. Preheat the oven to 350°F.
2. In a medium bowl, combine ⅓ cup of the rosemary, fennel seeds, 1½ teaspoons of pepper, garlic, lemon juice, soy sauce and 2 tablespoons of oil.
3. Place the chicken breast side up in a roasting pan. Gently slide your fingers under the skin and rub a thick layer of the rosemary mixture so that the skin remains.
4. Spread the rest of the rosemary mixture and add the lemon juice zest to the cavity of the chicken.
5. Grill the chicken for 2½ hours or until a thermometer on the inside of the thigh reads 165°F. Remove from the oven, cover with aluminium foil and let stand for 10 minutes.
6. Prepare the mixture towards the end of cooking: Heat the remaining 4 teaspoons of oil in a large skillet over medium heat.
7. Add the sweet potatoes and the remaining 2 tablespoons of rosemary and sauté for 5 minutes; cover and cook for another 8 minutes.
8. Add the onion, zucchini, yellow squash and the remaining ½ teaspoon of pepper. Cover and cook, 7 to 8 minutes, until the yellow squash is tender.

Serving Suggestion: Serve the Lemon Chicken with Sautéed Squash with soup.

Variation Tip: Use turkey breast in case not having chicken breast.

Nutritional Information Per Serving:

Calories 510| Fat 18g |Sodium 325mg | Carbs 43g | Fibre 6g | Sugar 6g | Protein 42g

Chicken Cutlets with White Wine Butter Sauce

Ingredients:

- 4 (5- to 6-ounce) boneless, skinless chicken breasts
- ¼ teaspoon each sea salt and ground black pepper
- 2 tablespoons whole-wheat flour
- 1 tablespoon safflower oil
- ¼ cup slivered unsalted almonds
- ½ cup dry white wine
- ¼ cup low-sodium chicken broth
- 2 tablespoons organic unsalted butter, chilled, cut into small pieces
- 2 green onions, thinly sliced

Prep Time:	15 minutes
Cook Time:	10 minutes
Serves:	4

Preparation:

1. Using a mallet or rolling pin, crush each chicken breast between 2 layers of cling film into ½-inch-thick chops. Season with salt and pepper.
2. Place the flour in a shallow bowl. Dip chicken in flour to coat both sides, shake off excess. Throw in the flour.
3. Heat the oil in a large skillet over medium heat. Add the cutlets and cook, turning them once, until golden brown on both sides and no longer pink on the inside, 3 to 4 minutes per side. Place on a plate and cover with foil.
4. Put the almonds in the pan and fry for 1 minute until golden, stirring constantly. Add the wine and broth and scrape the golden pieces from the pan with a wooden spoon.
5. Cook, stirring occasionally, until slightly thickened, 1 to 1½ minutes. Remove from the heat and gradually add the butter until it melts and the sauce thickens. Add the onions. Divide the chicken between plates and distribute the sauce evenly on top.

Serving Suggestion: Serve the Chicken Cutlets with White Wine Butter Sauce with salad.

Variation Tip: Use almond flour in case not having whole wheat flour.

Nutritional Information Per Serving:

Calories 381| Fat 17g |Sodium 195mg | Carbs 5g | Fibre 1g | Sugar 1g | Protein 38g

Sticky Honey Garlic Chicken Wings

Ingredients:

- 3 tablespoons each raw honey and fresh orange juice
- 2 tablespoons each Sucanat, reduced-sodium soy sauce, hot sauce, rice vinegar and fresh lime juice
- 1 teaspoon toasted sesame oil
- 2 teaspoons grated ginger
- 2 cloves garlic, minced
- 1 teaspoon arrowroot starch
- 2 pounds split chicken wings
- chopped fresh cilantro for garnish, optional

Prep Time:	15 minutes
Cook Time:	40 minutes
Serves:	4

Preparation:

1. Preheat the oven to 440°F and line a large baking sheet with parchment paper.
2. Prepare the sauce: Combine honey, orange juice, Sucanat, soy sauce, hot sauce, vinegar, lime juice, oil, ginger and garlic in a medium saucepan. Hit the arrow. Place the pot over medium heat and cook, stirring constantly, until the sauce thickens, about 1 to 2 minutes. Let cool to room temperature.
3. Keep ¼ cup of the sauce in a separate bowl for soaking. Place the chicken wings on the prepared dish and brush with the sauce from the pan.
4. Bake for 20 minutes and turn over, pouring the rest of the sauce from the pan over them. Bake an additional 18 to 20 minutes until the thermometer reads 165°F when inserted into the thickest (boneless) part. Transferred to a plate; Garnish with cilantro.
5. Pour ¼ cup of the reserved sauce over the wings or use as a sauce (reheat if desired). Garnish with cilantro (if using).

Serving Suggestion: Serve the Sticky Honey Garlic Chicken Wings with salad.

Variation Tip: Use maple syrup in case not having honey.

Nutritional Information Per Serving:

Calories 217| Fat 11g |Sodium 285mg | Carbs 13g | Fibre 0.6g | Sugar 16g | Protein 16.8g

Pesto Pasta with Ground Turkey

Ingredients:

- ½ pound whole wheat rotini pasta (you can use whatever shape you have)
- 1 pound ground turkey
- 1 teaspoon garlic powder
- a big pinch coarse salt and fresh ground pepper
- 2 large handfuls kale, chopped into small pieces
- ¾ to 1 cup prepared pesto
- ½ cup crumbled feta (use more if you like)

Preparation:

1. Cook pasta according to directions.
2. While the noodles are cooking, sauté the turkey in a large non-stick skillet over medium heat. Season the turkey with garlic powder, salt and pepper.
3. Add the chopped kale and continue cooking for 5 to 7 minutes until smooth. Add ¼ cup of pasta water to the turkey and kale mixture. Season with a little salt and pepper. Turn off the heat when the kale is tender.
4. When the noodles are ready, use a large slotted spoon to add the cooked noodles to the turkey and kale mixture in a saucepan (or drain the noodles in the sink and add the drained noodles).
5. Add the pesto to the pasta, turkey and kale and mix until well combined. Add the feta and stir gently.
6. Serve with sliced tomatoes and Kalamata olives.

Prep Time:	10 minutes
Cook Time:	20 minutes
Serves:	4

Serving Suggestion: Serve the Pesto Pasta with Ground Turkey with salad.

Variation Tip: Use gluten free pasta in case not having whole wheat rotini pasta

Nutritional Information Per Serving:

Calories 211| Fat 11.2g |Sodium 155mg | Carbs 19.3g | Fibre 13.6g | Sugar 6g | Protein 16.8g

Spicy Ground Turkey Stir-Fried with Green Bean

Ingredients:

- 1 pound green beans
- 4 teaspoons coconut oil (or vegetable oil)
- 1 tablespoon sesame oil
- 2 garlic cloves, minced
- 2 tablespoons ginger, minced
- 2 pounds 99% lean ground turkey
- 4 tablespoons low sodium soy sauce
- 2 tablespoons rice vinegar
- 2 teaspoons Asian chili garlic paste
- sambal oelek

Prep Time:	05 minutes
Cook Time:	20 minutes
Serves:	4

Preparation:

1. Preheat the oven to broil.
2. Toss the green beans with half the coconut oil. Place on a baking sheet lined with foil. Roast for 6 to 8 minutes until tender and starting to char. Shake the pan once during cooking.
3. Meanwhile, heat the rest of the coconut and sesame oil over medium heat. Add the ground turkey, garlic and ginger. Sauté until turkey is cooked through.
4. Add the green beans to the pan and stir. Then add the soy sauce, rice vinegar and sambal oelek. Cook for 1 minute. Season to taste and, if necessary, season with additional soy sauce.

Serving Suggestion: Serve the Spicy Ground Turkey Sir-Fried with Green Bean with rice.

Variation Tip: Use coconut aminos in case not having soy sauce.

Nutritional Information Per Serving:

Calories 294| Fat 12g |Sodium 725mg | Carbs 11g | Fibre 4g | Sugar 4g | Protein 39g

Chicken Fried Rice with Pineapple

Ingredients:

- 2 cups short-grain brown rice
- 2 tablespoons minced lemongrass
- 1½ teaspoons fish sauce
- 2 teaspoons reduced-sodium soy sauce
- 2 teaspoons Sriracha
- 8 ounces boneless, skinless chicken breast, thinly sliced
- ¼ teaspoon ground white pepper
- 3 tablespoons coconut oil, divided
- 2 tablespoons minced fresh cilantro stems
- 4 teaspoons chopped garlic
- 1½ cups sliced green beans (1-inch slices)
- 1 cup stemmed and thinly sliced shiitake mushrooms
- 1 cup peeled and chopped fresh pineapple (½-inch pieces)
- ½ cup chopped seeded tomato
- ¼ cup thinly sliced green onions
- 1 cup loosely packed torn fresh Thai basil

Prep Time:	25 minutes
Cook Time:	55 minutes
Serves:	6

Preparation:

1. In a medium pot, bring the rice, lemongrass and 4 cups of water to a boil.
2. Reduce heat, cover and simmer until rice is tender, about 45 minutes.
3. Remove from the heat and let stand, covered, for 5 minutes.
4. Transfer the rice to a rimmed baking sheet and refrigerate for about 1 hour until cool to the touch. (Note: do not skip the cooling step; using hot rice in the recipe will cause it to boil and become sticky.)
5. In a small bowl, combine the fish sauce, soy sauce and Siracha; put aside. Toss the chicken with the pepper. In a wok or large skillet, heat 1 tablespoon of oil over high heat. Add the chicken and sauté for about 2 minutes until cooked through. Transferred to a plate.
6. In the same wok, heat 1 tablespoon of oil over medium heat. Add the coriander stems and garlic and sauté for 20 seconds.
7. Add the beans and mushrooms and sauté for about 2 minutes, until the beans are tender but crisp. Slide to one side of the wok.
8. Pour 1 tablespoon of remaining oil on the empty side of the wok and add the rice. Cook for 30 seconds without stirring to brown the rice a little, then brown for 30 seconds.
9. Add the mixture of chicken, pineapple, tomato, onion and fish sauce and sauté for 1 minute.
10. Remove the wok from the heat, add the basil and stir once.

Serving Suggestion: Serve the Chicken Fried Rice with Pineapple with salad.

Variation Tip: Use turkey in case not having chicken.

Nutritional Information Per Serving:

Calories 346| Fat 12g |Sodium 352mg | Carbs 59.3g | Fibre 3.6g | Sugar 6g | Protein 16.8g

Beef and Lamb Recipes

Beef-Stuffed Peppers

Ingredients:

- 1 tablespoon olive oil
- large bell peppers (red, orange, or yellow have the best flavor.)
- 1 pound ground beef
- ½ cup onions, finely minced
- 1 tablespoon garlic, finely minced
- 1 cup carrots, finely minced
- 1 cup cauliflower rice
- 2 cups tomato sauce (leave 6 tablespoons off to the side!)
- 3 tablespoons fresh basil chopped finely
- 2 tablespoons fresh parsley chopped finely
- ½ teaspoon pepper
- ½ teaspoon salt

Prep Time:	15 minutes
Cook Time:	4 minutes
Serves:	4

Preparation:

1. Heat the olive oil in a large frying pan. Fry the beef for 5 to 10 minutes.
2. While the beef is cooking, cut off the tops of the peppers and remove the seeds.
3. Add the mixture of onions, garlic and carrots to the beef. Make sure to set the cauliflower rice aside, you don't want it to cook!
4. Fry until the vegetables are tender. When everything is done, turn off the heat. Add the raw cauliflower rice, tomato sauce and seasonings.
5. Fill the peppers with the mixture and cover each pepper with the remaining tablespoon of tomato sauce. You can use a spoon or your hands to fill the peppers and push the mixture down so that everything fits inside.
6. Place the peppers in the slow cooker and ¼ cup of water in the bottom. Cook the peppers over low heat for 4 to 6 hours.

Serving Suggestion: Serve the Beef-Stuffed Peppers with rice.

Variation Tip: Use coconut aminos in case not having soy sauce.

Nutritional Information Per Serving:

Calories 294| Fat 12g |Sodium 725mg | Carbs 11g | Fibre 4g | Sugar 4g | Protein 39g

Korean Beef

Ingredients:

- 1 tablespoon sesame oil
- 1 pound ground beef
- 3 cloves garlic minced
- ¼ cup coconut sugar (add more if you like it sweeter)
- ¼ cup soy sauce
- ½ teaspoon fresh ginger minced (see note)
- ½ to 1 teaspoon crushed red pepper, depending on how spicy you like it
- salt and pepper
- ½ cup sliced green onions

Prep Time:	05 minutes
Cook Time:	10 minutes
Serves:	6

Preparation:

1. Heat a large skillet over medium heat. Brown the minced meat in sesame oil.
2. Add the garlic towards the end of the cooking time and cook for a few minutes. Let the fat drain.
3. Add the brown sugar, soy sauce, ginger, salt and pepper, and red pepper. Simmer for a few minutes to combine the flavors.
4. Serve over steamed rice and garnish with spring onions. If you go for a low carb option, it also goes great with a salad!

Serving Suggestion: Serve the Korean Beef with rice.

Variation Tip: Use coconut amions in case not having soy sauce.

Nutritional Information Per Serving:

Calories 394| Fat 20g |Sodium 525mg | Carbs 13g | Fibre 4g | Sugar 9.4g | Protein 29g

Healthy Beef and Broccoli

Ingredients:

- 2 pounds beef, you can use: steak tips, thinly sliced skirt steak, flank steak, or sirloin cut in small 1-inch cubes
- 12 ounces broccoli
- 3 cups cauliflower rice

For the Marinade:

- ½ cup coconut aminos
- ½ cup beef broth
- 2 tablespoons rice wine vinegar
- ⅓ cup honey
- 1 tablespoon fresh garlic, minced
- ½ tablespoon fresh ginger, grated
- 1 teaspoon pepper
- 1 tablespoon sesame seeds, optional

Prep Time:	10 minutes
Cook Time:	6 hours 20 min
Serves:	4

Preparation:

1. Combine the marinade in a bowl. To marinate in a slow cooker. Add meat until covered.
2. Cook over low heat for 6 hours.
3. After cooking, remove the liquid from the slow cooker and pour it into a large pot on the stovetop. Bring the sauce to a boil. Cook on high heat for 15 minutes. The sauce should be simmering and bubbly all the time. Beat occasionally to prevent the sauce from burning.
4. While the sauce is cooking, cook the broccoli. Place in a microwave-safe bowl with ¼ cup of water and place in the microwave for 3 to 4 minutes on the highest setting.
5. While the broccoli is cooking, lightly brown the cauliflower rice in a pan with 1 teaspoon of olive oil.
6. Once the sauce has thickened, add the cooked meat to the pan and stir to coat it with the sauce. You can shred the steak by squeezing it gently while stirring if you want more shredded meat. It should collapse easily.
7. Assemble bowls with cauliflower rice, broccoli and beef.

Serving Suggestion: Serve the Beef and Broccoli with rice or cauliflower rice.

Variation Tip: Use maple syrup in case not having honey.

Nutritional Information Per Serving:

Calories 770| Fat 32g |Sodium 225mg | Carbs 31g | Fibre 4g | Sugar 24g | Protein 44g

Moroccan Lamb Tagine

Ingredients:

- 2 pounds boneless lamb roast, cut into 1-inch pieces
- kosher salt
- 3 cups low-sodium chicken broth
- 1 cup dried apricots
- 3 tablespoons extra-virgin olive oil
- 1 onion, chopped
- 4 cloves garlic, sliced
- 2 teaspoons freshly minced ginger
- 2 tablespoons tomato paste
- 1 cinnamon stick
- a small pinch of saffron
- ½ teaspoon ground turmeric
- ½ teaspoon ground coriander
- ¼ teaspoon ground cardamom
- ¼ teaspoon ground nutmeg
- ¼ teaspoon ground cloves
- freshly ground black pepper
- ¼ cup freshly chopped cilantro, plus more for garnish
- ½ cup toasted almond slivers

Prep Time:	20 minutes
Cook Time:	2 hours 20 minutes.
Serves:	8

Preparation:

1. In a large bowl, toss the lamb with about 2 teaspoons of salt. Let stand in the refrigerator at room temperature for 1 hour or overnight.
2. In a small saucepan over medium heat, bring the chicken broth to a boil. Remove from the heat and add the dried apricots. Let stand for at least 15 minutes.
3. Heat the oil in a tagine or Dutch oven over medium heat. Add the lamb and cook until golden brown, about 4 minutes per side. Work in batches as needed. Take the lamb out of the pot and place it on a plate.
4. Reduce the heat to medium and add the onion to the pot. Cook 5 minutes until tender.
5. Add the garlic and ginger and cook until fragrant 1 minute more, then add the tomato paste and stir until covered. Add the cinnamon stick, saffron and spices and cook for another 1 minute until toasted.
6. Add the lamb, apricots and broth to the pot and season with salt and pepper. Bring to a boil, then reduce the heat and simmer, covered, until the lamb is tender and the liquid has reduced, about 1 hour 30 minutes.
7. Remove from the heat and add the cilantro. Garnish with toasted almonds, mint and more cilantro. Serve over hot couscous.

Serving Suggestion: Serve the Moroccan Lamb Tagine with couscous.

Variation Tip: Use dried peaches in case not having dried apricots.

Nutritional Information Per Serving:

Calories 294| Fat 12g |Sodium 725mg | Carbs 11g | Fibre 4g | Sugar 4g | Protein 39g

Grilled Flank Steak with Mustardy Potato Salad

Ingredients:

- 1½ pounds small new potatoes, halved if large
- ¼ cup freshly chopped chives, plus additional for garnish
- 1 tablespoon yellow mustard
- 1 tablespoon apple cider vinegar
- 3 tablespoons extra-virgin olive oil, divided
- kosher salt
- freshly ground black pepper
- 1¼ pounds flank steak, cut into 2 pieces
- 1 teaspoon ground coriander

Prep Time:	10 minutes
Cook Time:	30 minutes
Serves:	4

Preparation:

1. Fill a large saucepan with 1 inch of water and place it in a steamer basket. Bring to a boil and cook the potatoes for 15 to 18 minutes until tender. Drain and transfer to a large bowl.
2. Toss with the chives, mustard, vinegar and 1 tablespoon of oil and season with salt and pepper.
3. Meanwhile, cook the steak. Heat the remaining 2 tablespoons of oil in a large skillet over medium heat. Season the steak with cilantro, salt and pepper.
4. Boil and turn once until an instant-read thermometer, inserted into the thickest part, reads 130°F for medium vintage, about 3 to 4 minutes per side.
5. Place on a cutting board and let stand 5 minutes, then cut into slices. Serve with potatoes and garnish with chives.

Serving Suggestion: Serve the Grilled Flank Steak with Mustardy Potato Salad with cauliflower rice.

Variation Tip: Use sweet potatoes in case not having potatoes.

Nutritional Information Per Serving:

Calories 394| Fat 22g |Sodium 525mg | Carbs 16g | Fibre 4g | Sugar 4g | Protein 29g

Taco-Stuffed Zucchini

Ingredients:

- 2 large zucchinis
- 1 tablespoon avocado oil
- ¾ pound lean ground beef
- 1 medium tomato, chopped
- 1 bunch scallions, sliced
- 1 tablespoon chili powder
- 2 teaspoons ground cumin
- ¾ teaspoon salt, divided
- ½ teaspoon garlic powder
- ¼ teaspoon ground pepper
- 2 tablespoons shredded Monterey Jack cheese
- 1 cup shredded romaine lettuce
- 1 avocado, chopped
- 2 tablespoons Pico de Gallo

Preparation:

1. Cut each zucchini in half lengthwise. Cut a thin slice from the bottom so that each half is flat. Remove the pulp, leaving a ¼-inch crust. Chop the pulp.
2. Heat the oil in a large skillet over medium heat. Add the meat, tomato, chives, chili powder, cumin, ½ teaspoon of salt and garlic powder. Cook and break the meat into small pieces until no longer pink, 5 to 6 minutes. Add the minced meat.
3. Meanwhile, place the prepared zucchini halves on a microwaveable plate; Sprinkle with the remaining ¼ teaspoon of salt and pepper. Cover and place in the microwave on high power for 2 to 3 minutes until crispy and tender. To discover.
4. Place the rack in the upper third of the oven.
5. Preheat the grill to high heat.
6. Place the zucchini halves on a baking sheet. Spread the meat filling over the zucchini halves and sprinkle each half with 2 tablespoons of cheese. Broil until cheese is melted, about 2 minutes.
7. Serve with salad, avocado and Pico de Gallo to taste.

Prep Time:	55 minutes
Cook Time:	20 minutes
Serves:	4

Serving Suggestion: Serve the Taco-Stuffed Zucchini with salad.

Variation Tip: Use Eggplant in case not having zucchini.

Nutritional Information Per Serving:

Calories 394| Fat 12g |Sodium 625mg | Carbs 14g | Fibre 7.4g | Sugar 5.4g | Protein 29g

Meatball Spaghetti Squash Boats

Ingredients:

- 2 medium spaghetti squashes about 4 pounds
- 1 cup shredded mozzarella
- 2 cups tomato sauce

For meatballs:

- 1 pound ground beef
- ½ cup almond meal
- ¼ cup onion finely chopped, I pulse mine in a food processor
- ½ tablespoon minced garlic
- ½ teaspoon dried parsley
- ½ teaspoon dried basil
- ½ teaspoon dried oregano
- 1 tablespoon olive oil
- ½ teaspoon salt
- ½ teaspoon pepper
- ¼ teaspoon red pepper flakes, optional

Prep Time:	05 minutes
Cook Time:	40 minutes
Serves:	4

Preparation:

1. Preheat the oven to 400°F. Prepare two baking sheets lined with parchment paper or a Silpat baking sheet.
2. Cut the spaghetti squash lengthwise, remove the seeds and place it on a baking sheet.
3. Drizzle the spaghetti squash with olive oil and open it. Bake for 20 minutes.
4. While the spaghetti squash is cooking, combine the dough with the meatballs in a bowl.
5. Roll ½-inch balls. Bake for 10 minutes.
6. While the meatballs are cooking, remove the spaghetti squash from the oven and remove it from the centre with a fork. Remove about half of the pumpkin from the skin.
7. When the meatballs are cooked, remove them from the baking sheet.
8. Combine cooked meatballs, grated spaghetti squash filling and tomato sauce in a bowl.
9. Fill the spaghetti squash skins with the mixture. Garnish with mozzarella and return to the oven for 10 to 12 minutes.
10. Optional: Turn the oven to grill/high for the last 2 minutes for a golden, crisp and cheesy surface.

Serving Suggestion: Serve the Meatball Spaghetti Squash Boats with salad.

Variation Tip: Use coconut flour in case not having almond meal.

Nutritional Information Per Serving:

Calories 458| Fat 17g |Sodium 525mg | Carbs 31g | Fibre 11g | Sugar 20g | Protein 40g

Garlic Lime Flank Steak

Ingredients:

- 2½ pounds flank steak
- 1½ tablespoons minced garlic
- 1 tablespoon lime zest
- ¼ cup lime juice
- ¼ cup olive oil
- ½ teaspoon salt
- ½ teaspoon pepper
- ½ teaspoon onion powder

Preparation:

1. Combine the marinade in a bowl.
2. Cover the rock steak with the marinade and marinate for at least 30 minutes, but no more than 8 hours.
3. When you're ready to cook, preheat the grill to medium-high heat. Put the steak on the grill. Cook 4 to 5 minutes, turn and cook another 4 to 5 minutes.
4. Cook until the internal temperature is 140°F for a medium steak and 150°F for a well done steak.
5. Remove the steak from the grill, cover with foil and let stand 5 minutes before cutting.
6. Cut the steak against the fibre and serve with grilled vegetables or salad.

Prep Time:	05 minutes
Cook Time:	10 minutes
Serves:	6

Serving Suggestion: Serve the Garlic Lime Flank Steak with salad.

Variation Tip: You can use dried garlic in place of fresh garlic.

Nutritional Information Per Serving:

Calories 304| Fat 14g |Sodium 225mg | Carbs 2g | Fibre 1g | Sugar 1g | Protein 41g

Ground Beef and Sweet Potato Chili

Ingredients:

- 1 tablespoon olive oil
- 2 pounds ground beef
- 1 cup onion diced finely
- 2 cups sweet potato cubes cut in 1-inch pieces
- 28 ounces tomatoes, crunched
- ½ teaspoon salt
- 1 teaspoon pepper
- 1 teaspoon chili powder
- ⅛ teaspoon cayenne pepper
- 1 teaspoon paprika
- 1 teaspoon garlic powder
- Optional toppings: avocado or guacamole

Prep Time:	05 minutes
Cook Time:	6 hour 10 minutes
Serves:	4

Preparation:

1. Heat the olive oil in a pan on the fire. Add minced meat and sauté until golden brown, about 10 minutes.
2. While the ground beef is cooking, chop the onions and sweet potatoes.
3. Add the onions to the minced meat and sauté for another 5 minutes.
4. Place the minced meat/golden onions in the slow cooker. Add the diced sweet potatoes, tomatoes and spices.
5. Cook over low heat for 6 hours or raised for 4 hours.
6. Garnish with avocado or guacamole.

Serving Suggestion: Serve the Ground Beef and Sweet Potato Chili with rice.

Variation Tip: Use fresh garlic in place of garlic powder.

Nutritional Information Per Serving:

Calories 394| Fat 18g |Sodium 500mg | Carbs 21g | Fibre 5g | Sugar 9g | Protein 34g

Instant Pot Beef Stew Recipe

Ingredients:

- 1 tablespoon olive oil
- 1 pound stew meat
- 1 tablespoon garlic, finely minced
- ½ cup onion, finely chopped
- 2 cups carrots cut in ½-inch-thick circles
- 1 cup celery thinly sliced ¼-inch-thick
- 2 cups fingerling or russet potatoes, cut in 1-inch pieces (about 8 ounces)
- 1 tablespoon tomato paste
- 1 bay leaf
- ¼ teaspoon salt
- ½ teaspoon pepper
- 1 teaspoon fresh rosemary, chopped
- 1 cup beef broth, low or no sodium
- ¼ cup red wine, optional
- 1 cup frozen peas

Prep Time:	05 minutes
Cook Time:	35 minutes
Serves:	4

Preparation:

1. Sear the instant pot for 10 minutes. Heat the olive oil. Brown the stew on all sides (about 5 minutes). Add onions/garlic and sauté for another 5 minutes.
2. While the meat/onions browning, chop all other vegetables/potatoes.
3. Once the meat is golden, add all the remaining ingredients EXCEPT the peas and stir until just combined.
4. Cover and set to seal, manual pressure for 25 minutes
5. It will take about 10 minutes for the instant pot to lower.
6. When you're done cooking, quickly release the pressure. Throw in the bay leaf, add the frozen peas and enjoy!

Serving Suggestion: Serve the Beef Stew with rice.

Variation Tip: You can use dried garlic in place of fresh garlic.

Nutritional Information Per Serving:

Calories 220| Fat 10g |Sodium 365mg | Carbs 2.1g | Fibre 6g | Sugar 8g | Protein 38g

Pork Recipes

Garlic Lime Pork Chops

Ingredients:

- 4 (6-ounce) each lean boneless pork chops
- 4 cloves garlic, crushed
- ½ teaspoon cumin
- ½ teaspoon chili powder
- ½ teaspoon paprika
- 1 tablespoon lime juice
- 1 teaspoon lime zest
- 1 teaspoon kosher salt and fresh pepper

Preparation:

1. Cut the fat off the pork. In a large bowl, season the pork with the garlic, cumin, chili powder, paprika, salt and pepper. Squeeze out the lime juice and some of the lime zest and marinate for at least 20 minutes.
2. Grill: Line roasting pan with foil for easy cleaning. Place the pork chops on the roasting pan and grill for about 4 to 5 minutes per side or until golden brown. For grilling, grill over medium heat for 4 to 5 minutes per side.

Prep Time:	05 minutes
Cook Time:	10 minutes
Serves:	4

Serving Suggestion: Serve the Garlic Lime Pork Chops with salad.

Variation Tip: Use sweet potatoes in case not having potatoes.

Nutritional Information Per Serving:

Calories 340| Fat 10g |Sodium 325mg | Carbs 21g | Fibre 6g | Sugar 8g | Protein 31g

Herb Crusted Pork Chops

Ingredients:

- 4 boneless pork chops, fat trimmed
- 2 tablespoons Dijon mustard
- ½ cup whole wheat Panko breadcrumbs
- 1 tablespoon fresh thyme, chopped
- 1 tablespoon fresh parsley, minced
- ⅛ teaspoon sea salt
- ⅛ teaspoon pepper
- 1 tablespoon olive oil

Preparation:

1. Preheat the oven to 450°F.
2. Rub mustard evenly over pork chops. Combine the panko, thyme, parsley, salt and pepper in a large bowl and toss the pork chops into the panko mixture.
3. Heat a large ovenproof skillet over medium heat. Add the oil to the pan and toss to coat. Add pork chops, sauté for 2 minutes or until golden brown.
4. Turn the pork over and place the pan in the oven for about 8 minutes or until the pork reaches 145°F or 63°C in the centre. Enjoy!

Prep Time:	05 minutes
Cook Time:	25 minutes
Serves:	4

Serving Suggestion: Serve the Herb crusted pork chops with cauliflower rice.

Variation Tip: Use normal breadcrumbs in case not wheat Panko breadcrumbs.

Nutritional Information Per Serving:

Calories 210| Fat 9.4g |Sodium 325mg | Carbs 5.1g | Fibre 0.6g | Sugar 8g | Protein 24.1g

Honey Chipotle Pork Roast

Ingredients:

- 2 tablespoons raw honey
- ½ teaspoon chipotle hot sauce
- 1 tablespoon chipotle puree
- 1 teaspoon cilantro
- ½ teaspoon salt
- 1 teaspoon chili powder
- 1 teaspoon cumin
- ¼ teaspoon black pepper
- 1 clove garlic, minced
- 2 pounds pork roast

Prep Time:	10 minutes
Cook Time:	1 hour 25minutes
Serves:	4

Preparation:

1. Preheat the oven to 350°F.
2. Place the roast pork in a buttered baking dish, white lid facing up.
3. Use a craft knife to cut a cross pattern on the roast through the layer of fat.
4. Whisk honey chipotle frosting in bowl and spread half over roast.
5. Bake for 40 minutes.
6. Brush the roast with the remaining frosting and bake an additional 35 to 40 minutes until it has reached an internal temperature of at least 145°F or 63°C.
7. Take out of the oven and let stand 5 to 10 minutes.
8. Cut and serve.

Serving Suggestion: Serve the Honey Chipotle Pork Roast with salad.

Variation Tip: Use maple syrup in case not having honey.

Nutritional Information Per Serving:

Calories 372| Fat 10g |Sodium 425mg | Carbs 19g | Fibre 1g | Sugar 18g | Protein 51g

Quinoa Fried Rice with Pork

Ingredients:

- 1 pound ground pork
- 2 eggs
- cups cooked quinoa
- 2 cups frozen vegetable mixture
- 2 tablespoons toasted sesame oil
- 2 tablespoons gluten-free soy sauce or coconut aminos
- 1 tablespoon Sriracha sauce
- 1 teaspoon ground ginger

Prep Time:	05 minutes
Cook Time:	10 minutes
Serves:	4

Preparation:

1. Heat the sesame oil over medium heat. Add the pork and cook until golden brown, about 3 minutes. Transfer to a plate and return the pot to the heat.
2. Add the egg, twist to coat the bottom and cook for 30 seconds until the edges start to brown and you can remove it from the pan.
3. Turn the egg over and cook until it no longer runs. Place on a cutting board and cut into ½-inch pieces.
4. Return the pork to the pan, add the quinoa and frozen vegetables. Stir in the sauces and ginger and stir until the vegetables are heated through and no longer frozen. Add the eggs and stir to combine.
5. Serve immediately.

Serving Suggestion: Serve the Quinoa Fried Rice with Pork with salad.

Variation Tip: Use rice in case not having quinoa.

Nutritional Information Per Serving:

Calories 554| Fat 10g |Sodium 411mg | Carbs 51g | Fibre 8g | Sugar 1g | Protein

One Pan Roasted Pork Tenderloin with Veggies

Ingredients:

- 2 pounds pork tenderloins (1 to 1½ pounds)
- ¼ cup honey
- 3 garlic cloves (minced on the microplate)
- 3 tablespoons coarsely ground mustard (deli mustard is fine)
- 3 to 4 sprigs of rosemary (removed from stem and finely chopped)
- 3 tablespoons white wine
- 3 tablespoons extra-virgin olive oil
- 1½ pounds Yukon Gold potatoes, unpeeled (quartered)
- 1 pound green beans (trimmed)
- salt and pepper
- pan spray

Prep Time:	05 minutes
Cook Time:	30 minutes
Serves:	8

Preparation:

1. Preheat the oven to 450°F.
2. Combine olive oil, honey, garlic, mustard, wine and rosemary in a bowl. Season to taste and season with salt and pepper as needed.
3. Pat the pork dry with paper towel and season with pepper. Brush fillets all around with icing
4. Spray skillet with skillet spray or brush with olive oil.
5. Arrange the green beans crosswise in the centre of the rimmed baking sheet, leaving room for the potatoes on both sides.
6. Place the potatoes upside down in the pan.
7. Spray the potatoes and green beans with cooking spray and season with S&P.
8. Place fillets side by side, intact, lengthwise over green beans. Brush the fillets with the glaze using a knife or pastry brush.
9. Grill until pork is 140°F, about 20 to 25 minutes.
10. Place the fillets on a cutting board, cover with foil and let stand while the vegetables finish cooking.
11. Increase the heat in the oven to 475°F and return the baking sheet to the oven and sauté until the vegetables are tender and golden, another 5 to 10 minutes.
12. Get out of the oven,
13. Transfer the vegetables to a plate. Cut the pork into ½-inch-thick slices and place them on top of the vegetables, pouring the juice accumulated over them. To serve.

Serving Suggestion: Serve the One Pan Roasted Pork Tenderloin with Veggies with rice.

Variation Tip: Use sweet potatoes in case not having potatoes.

Nutritional Information Per Serving:

Calories 340| Fat 10g |Sodium 325mg | Carbs 21g | Fibre 6g | Sugar 8g | Protein 31g

Pork Chops with Balsamic Peppers

Ingredients:

- 4 centre cut pork chops
- ½ teaspoon salt
- ½ teaspoon freshly ground black pepper
- 1 tablespoon extra-virgin olive oil
- 1½ teaspoons chopped fresh rosemary, divided
- 3 garlic cloves, thinly sliced
- 1 red bell pepper, cut into 1½-inch strips
- 1 yellow (or orange) bell pepper, cut into 1½-inch strips
- 2 teaspoons balsamic vinegar

Preparation:

1. Heat a large skillet over medium heat. Sprinkle the pork with salt and pepper.
2. Add the oil to the pan and turn to coat. Place the pork in the pan and brown for 7 minutes.
3. Reduce the heat to medium and turn the pork. Add 1 teaspoon of rosemary, garlic and paprika, cook for 9 minutes or until the peppers are tender and the pork is cooked.
4. Drizzle with balsamic vinegar and sprinkle with the remaining ½ teaspoon of rosemary. Serve and enjoy!

Prep Time:	05 minutes
Cook Time:	25 minutes
Serves:	4

Serving Suggestion: Serve the Pork Chops with Balsamic Peppers with cauliflower rice.

Variation Tip: Use thyme in case not rosemary.

Nutritional Information Per Serving:

Calories 210| Fat 10.1g |Sodium 325mg | Carbs 5g | Fibre 1.6g | Sugar 8g | Protein 25g

Seafood Recipes

Teriyaki Salmon Recipe

Ingredients:

- 2 ounces salmon fillet
- ¼ cup teriyaki sauce (recipe below)

Teriyaki Sauce

- ½ cup tamari sauce
- ¼ cup water
- ½ teaspoon powdered ginger
- 2 tablespoons white wine vinegar
- 1 teaspoon garlic powder
- 2 tablespoons pure maple syrup
- 1 tablespoon arrowroot powder

Prep Time:	05 minutes
Cook Time:	10 minutes
Serves:	2

Preparation:

Teriyaki Sauce

1. In a small to medium bowl, combine and whisk all the ingredients together.
2. Let stand in the refrigerator for 1 hour, then whisk again.
3. Transfer to a container and store in the refrigerator for up to 2 weeks.
4. We can freeze this sauce in ice cube trays for up to 6 months.

Salmon

1. Marinate the salmon in the sauce in the refrigerator for 20 minutes.
2. Place raw salmon on a large piece of foil.
3. Turn the side of the foil to prevent the sauce from dripping.
4. For the marinade sauce on the salmon.
5. Wrap the foil so you can move the salmon without losing the sauce.
6. Place the foil on a hot grill and cook for about 10 minutes.
7. Remove, open foil and serve.

Serving Suggestion: Serve the Teriyaki Salmon with cauliflower rice.

Variation Tip: Use soy sauce in case not tamari sauce.

Nutritional Information Per Serving:

Calories 274| Fat 11g |Sodium 1325mg | Carbs 5g | Fibre 1.6g | Sugar 8g | Protein 36g

Tuna Burgers

Ingredients:

- 8 ounces canned tuna (drained)
- ½ cup oat flour
- 2 large eggs
- ¼ cup minced celery
- ¼ cup minced red onion
- 1 tablespoon minced garlic
- 1 tablespoon prepared yellow mustard
- ½ teaspoon ground black pepper

Preparation:

1. Preheat your fryer to 350°F.
2. Put all the ingredients in a bowl and knead with your hands to form a good "dough".
3. Divide it into four equal parts and shape your patties. Make sure to press them flat so that they are even. They won't cook as well if they're rounder. So flatter them to make real burgers.
4. Put them on your air fryer tray or drawer
5. Cook for 15 minutes, turning halfway through cooking.
6. Prepare and serve your burger as usual.

Prep Time:	05 minutes
Cook Time:	25 minutes
Serves:	4

Serving Suggestion: Serve the Tuna Burgers with salad.

Variation Tip: Use salmon in case not tuna.

Nutritional Information Per Serving:

Calories 157| Fat 4g |Sodium 225mg | Carbs 15g | Fibre 1.6g | Sugar 1g | Protein 15g

Spicy Orange Shrimp Recipe

Ingredients:

- 1 pound small shrimp
- 2 teaspoons olive oil
- 1 tablespoon orange zest
- ¼ teaspoon ground cinnamon
- ¼ teaspoon cayenne pepper

Preparation:

1. Thaw and peel the shrimp. Thaw them by running them under cold water for a few minutes. Dry the peeled shrimp by draining them on a paper towel.
2. Place all the ingredients in a large skillet and brown the shrimp until heated through.

Prep Time:	10 minutes
Cook Time:	15 minutes
Serves:	4

Serving Suggestion: Serve the Spicy Orange Shrimp with cauliflower rice.

Variation Tip: Use lemon in case not orange.

Nutritional Information Per Serving:

Calories 133| Fat 4g |Sodium 825mg | Carbs 5g | Fibre 1g | Sugar 1g | Protein 23g

Walnut Crusted Cod

Ingredients:

- 1 pound wild cod (fresh or frozen/thawed)
- ¾ cup walnut pieces
- 1 teaspoon onion powder
- 1 tablespoon. F lemon zest
- fresh lemon wedges for serving
- fresh parsley for garnish, chopped
- salt as needed after cooking

Preparation:

1. Put the walnuts in a food processor and mix until you have a nice meal of almonds. It doesn't need to be ground too finely, just evenly ground. You don't really want to go overboard with the processor or you might end up with nut butter.

Prep Time:	15 minutes
Cook Time:	30 minutes
Serves:	4

2. Add the onion powder and lemon zest and mix several times with the food processor to combine.
3. Place the fish on a plate and cover with the nut filling. It gets a little wet and sticky, but it's still doable. It does not have to completely cover the fillet or both sides of the fish (it does not cook properly). It's meant to be a garnish, not breadcrumbs.
4. When the top of the cod is coated, place it in a baking dish.
5. Bake at 350°F for about 20 to 25 minutes or until the fish is cooked through. The cooking time varies slightly depending on the oven.
6. Then turn the oven on to toast and continue cooking for another 5 to 10 minutes, or until the nuts are golden brown from roasting.
7. Put on a plate, cool a little.
8. Serve with fresh lemon juice (wedges) and chopped fresh parsley for garnish.
9. Season with salt if needed.

Serving Suggestion: Serve the Walnut Crusted Cod with salad.

Variation Tip: Use pecans in case not walnuts.

Nutritional Information Per Serving:

Calories 323| Fat 20g |Sodium 85mg | Carbs 5g | Fibre 1.6g | Sugar 8g | Protein 31g

Popcorn Shrimp

Ingredients:

- 1 pound peeled, deveined, tail-off large shrimp (frozen is fine if you thaw)
- ½ cup shredded coconut
- ½ cup whole wheat Panko bread crumbs
- 1½ teaspoons garlic powder
- 1½ teaspoons onion powder
- 2 large egg whites
- 2 teaspoons coconut oil

Preparation:

1. Preheat the oven to 350°F.
2. Pat the shrimp dry with a paper towel if they are damp or wet.
3. In a medium mixing bowl, combine coconut flakes, breadcrumbs, garlic and onion powder.
4. Place the shrimp in the egg white and mix well.
5. Remove them (I used my hands), drain some of the excess and place them in the dried coconut mixture.
6. Shake until covered, then place one at a time on a parchment-lined baking sheet.
7. Bake for 20 minutes (no more!). They should be lightly browned.

Prep Time:	15 minutes
Cook Time:	20 minutes
Serves:	4

Serving Suggestion: Serve the Popcorn Shrimp with ketchup.

Variation Tip: Use normal bread crumbs in case not Panko bread crumbs.

Nutritional Information Per Serving:

Calories 263| Fat 11g |Sodium 925mg | Carbs 15g | Fibre 1.6g | Sugar 2g | Protein 27g

Brazilian Fish Stew

Ingredients:

Fish:

- 1 to 1½ pounds firm white fish-halibut, black cod, sea bass (thicker cuts are best)
- ½ teaspoon salt
- one lime, zest and juice

Stew/ Sauce:

- 2 to 3 tablespoons coconut oil
- 1 onion, finely diced
- ½ teaspoon salt
- 1 cup carrot, diced
- 1 red bell pepper, diced
- garlic cloves, rough chopped
- ½ jalapeno, finely diced
- 1 tablespoon tomato paste
- 2 teaspoons paprika
- 1 teaspoon ground cumin
- 1 cup fish or chicken stock
- 1 ½ cups tomatoes, diced
- a 14-ounce can coconut milk
- more salt to taste
- ½ cup chopped cilantro, scallions or Italian parsley
- squeeze of lime

Prep Time:	20 minutes
Cook Time:	20 minutes
Serves:	4

Preparation:

1. Rinse the fish, dry it and cut it into 2-cm pieces. Put in a bowl. Add the salt, the zest of half the lime and 1 tablespoon of the lime juice. Massage lightly to fully cover all parts. Put aside.
2. In a large skillet, heat olive oil over medium heat. Add the onion and salt and cook 2 to 3 minutes.
3. Reduce the heat to medium, add the carrot, bell pepper, garlic and jalapeño and cook for another 4 to 5 minutes.
4. Add the tomato paste, spices and broth. Mix and bring to a boil and add the tomatoes. Cover and simmer over low to medium heat for 5 minutes or until carrots are tender.
5. Add the coconut milk and season to taste and add more salt if necessary.
6. Put the fish in the stew and simmer for about 4 to 6 minutes until cooked through. Pour the flavourful coconut broth over the fish and cook to the desired doneness or longer for thicker pieces. (You can also finish this in a 350°F oven.)
7. Season and adjust the salt and squeeze with lime.

8. Serve over rice to serve, sprinkle with cilantro or chives and drizzle with lime.
9. Drizzle with a little olive oil if you wish.

Serving Suggestion: Serve the Brazilian Fish Stew with cauliflower rice.

Variation Tip: Use almond milk in case not coconut milk.

Nutritional Information Per Serving:

Calories 404| Fat 19.1g |Sodium 525mg | Carbs 15g | Fibre 2.6g | Sugar 4.8g | Protein 45g

Lemon Garlic Baked Salmon with Asparagus

Ingredients:

- 4 to 6 (6-ounce or 170 g) salmon fillets, skin removed
- 2 tablespoons minced garlic
- 2 tablespoons fresh chopped parsley
- ⅓ cup freshly squeezed lemon juice
- olive oil cooking spray
- 1 teaspoon kosher salt (or sea salt flakes)
- ½ teaspoon cracked black pepper
- bunches asparagus (24 spears), woody ends removed
- 1 lemon, sliced to garnish
- ⅓ cup beans/peas or any other greens

Preparation:

Prep Time:	05 minutes
Cook Time:	25 minutes
Serves:	6

1. Preheat the grill (or grill) to 400°F. Cover a baking sheet with foil. Place the oven rack on the second top rack (about 20 cm from the resistance).
2. Place the salmon on a large baking sheet. Rub each fillet evenly with garlic and parsley to evenly coat them over lemon juice. Drizzle with a thin layer of olive oil spray and season with salt and pepper. Arrange the asparagus and vegetables in a single layer around the salmon and cover with lemon wedges.
3. Broil (or broil) 8 to 10 minutes, or until the salmon is cooked to your liking (we think 8 minutes is great when the oven is hot).
4. Serve with asparagus and beans / peas and these crispy mashed potatoes!

Serving Suggestion: Serve the Lemon Garlic Baked Salmon with Asparagus with mashed potatoes.

Variation Tip: Use dried garlic powder in case not fresh garlic.

Nutritional Information Per Serving:

Calories 210| Fat 10.1g |Sodium 325mg | Carbs 5g | Fibre 1.6g | Sugar 8g | Protein 25g

Tuna Stuffed Avocado

Ingredients:

- 1 (5-ounce) can water packed tuna, drained
- 2 tablespoons clean mayo or Greek yogurt, if you don't mind the tang
- 1 pinch dried dill, to taste
- salt and pepper, to taste
- 1 medium avocado

Preparation:

1. In a small bowl, combine the tuna, mayonnaise or Greek yogurt and dill.
2. Season to taste with salt and pepper.
3. Fill the avocado halves with the tuna salad and serve.

Prep Time:	10 minutes
Cook Time:	00 minutes
Serves:	1

Serving Suggestion: Serve the Tuna Stuffed Avocado with soup.

Variation Tip: Use salmon in case not tuna.

Nutritional Information Per Serving:

Calories 565| Fat 45g |Sodium 550mg | Carbs 15g | Fibre 10g | Sugar 1g | Protein 31g

Pan Seared Salmon with Chia Seeds

Ingredients:

Pan Seared Salmon

- 2 (4 to 6 ounces) wild salmon or steelhead filets
- ½ teaspoon salt
- ¼ teaspoon pepper
- ½ teaspoon dried mint, dill or tarragon
- ½ teaspoon granulated garlic
- 2 teaspoons chia seeds
- 1 tablespoon olive oil
- ½ lemon, to finish

Fennel Slaw:

- 1 large fennel bulb, very thinly sliced (a mandolin is great for this)
- 1 Turkish cucumber
- ¼ cup thinly sliced sweet onion
- ½ ounce package dill or tarragon
- 2 tablespoons olive oil
- 2 to 3 tablespoon lemon juice
- salt and pepper to taste

Prep Time:	20 minutes
Cook Time:	10 minutes
Serves:	2

Preparation:

1. Make the slaw. Put the slaw ingredients in a medium bowl and mix well, adding salt and lemon. Put aside.
2. Brush the top of the salmon with olive oil.
3. Put the salt, pepper, dried herbs, garlic granules, chia seeds in a small bowl and mix.
4. Liberally brush the top of the fish with the chia mixture and press well to the edge with your fingers.
5. Heat the olive oil in a pan over medium heat. Let the pan heat up.
6. Add the fish with the chia seeds side down and sauté in the pan for 3 to 4 minutes until golden and crisp. Use a metal spatula to gently flip to keep the crust intact and continue cooking until the fish is cooked to the desired degree, 3 to 4 minutes or more depending on thickness.
7. Divide the fennel salad between two plates and place the fish on top. Squeeze with lemon and garnish with pickled red onions and fresh dill.

Serving Suggestion: Serve the Salmon with Chia Seeds with cauliflower rice.

Variation Tip: Use tuna in case not having salmon.

Nutritional Information Per Serving:

Calories 399| Fat 27.1g |Sodium 725mg | Carbs 11.5g | Fibre 2.6g | Sugar 6.8g | Protein 30.3g

Coconut Lemongrass Scallops with Lime

Ingredients:

- 1 shallot, finely diced
- 4 tablespoons white vinegar
- 1 stalk of fresh lemongrass (about 4 to 5 inches), smashed
- 2 thin slices ginger
- 1 can coconut milk
- 1 large lime, zest and juice
- 1½ teaspoons fish sauce, plus more to taste
- few slices red chili (optional)
- 1 to 1¼ pound large scallops
- 1 tablespoon coconut oil for searing
- salt and pepper
- leaves of fresh basil, cut into thin ribbons
- cooked rice and Sriracha
- kaffir lime leaves (optional)

Prep Time:	10 minutes
Cook Time:	15 minutes
Serves:	4

Preparation:

1. Put a small pot of rice on the heat to boil. In a small saucepan, simmer the marinated shallot over low heat until the vinegar is almost completely reduced, about 5 minutes.
2. Add the coconut milk, half the lime zest (keep the rest for garnish), crushed lemongrass and ginger and simmer over medium heat for 5 minutes. Don't overcook.
3. Add 1½ teaspoons of fish sauce and 1 tablespoon of lemon juice, turn off the heat and season to taste. Garnish with more lime or fish sauce if desired.
4. Add a few slices of fresh red pepper to warm them up. Set aside and let the flavor soak in while the rice cooks.
5. Rinse the scallops and dry them gently. Season with salt and pepper.
6. Heat the coconut oil in a pan over medium heat. When the pan is hot, add the scallops and sauté 2 to 3 minutes on each side (depending on size). When it's ready to your taste, set aside and sprinkle with lime. When ready to serve, heat the sauce slightly and strain.
7. Collect the bowls. Distribute the rice, cover with scallops, then pour the spicy lemongrass and coconut sauce over it, garnish with slices of fresh basil and the rest of the lime zest.
8. Enjoy!

Serving Suggestion: Serve the Coconut Lemongrass Scallops with Lime with cauliflower rice.

Variation Tip: Use soy milk in case not having coconut milk.

Nutritional Information Per Serving:

Calories 510| Fat 23g |Sodium 1325mg | Carbs 45g | Fibre 0.6g | Sugar 1.8g | Protein 35g

Salmon Chowder

Ingredients:

- 2 to 3 tablespoons olive oil (or butter)
- 1 onion, diced
- 1 small fennel bulb
- 1 cup celery, sliced
- 2 to 4 garlic cloves, rough chopped
- 1 teaspoon fennel seeds (optional)
- ½ teaspoon thyme dry, or 2 teaspoons fresh
- ½ teaspoon smoked paprika
- ⅓ cup vermouth, cooking sherry or white wine
- 2 cups fish or chicken stock, if using chicken broth see notes, on how to enhance
- ¾ pound baby potatoes, thinly sliced
- 1 teaspoon salt
- 1 bay leaf
- 1 pound skinless salmon, cut into 1- to 2-inch pieces
- 2 cups whole milk
- garnish: fennel fronds, lemon wedges, fresh dill or tarragon

Prep Time:	10 minutes
Cook Time:	25 minutes
Serves:	6

Preparation:

1. Heat the oil over medium heat and sauté the onion, fennel and celery for 5 to 6 minutes until fragrant.
2. Add the garlic, fennel seeds and thyme and sauté for two more minutes. Add the smoked paprika powder.
3. Add the vermouth and cook for about 1 to 2 minutes. Add the broth, salt, thyme and bay leaf and simmer over high heat. Add the potatoes and stir. Bring to a boil, cover and cook over medium heat until tender, about 8 to 10 minutes (check after 7 minutes, be careful not to cook for too long). While cooking, prepare the salmon.
4. Cut the salmon into 2-inch pieces, removing the brown fat (see notes) and bones. Sprinkle lightly with salt.
5. When the potatoes are tender, add the milk and simmer (do not boil) and add the salmon and poach in the soup for about 2 minutes. To put out the fire. The fish will continue to cook. Simmering the soup longer can cause it to curdle slightly. (Don't worry, it's still edible, but not quite as nice.) Use a fork to cut the fish into bite-sized pieces.
6. Season to taste, season to taste and serve immediately.
7. Garnish with fennel leaves, lemon wedges, fresh dill or tarragon.

Serving Suggestion: Serve the Salmon Chowder with cauliflower rice

Variation Tip: Use Thyme in case not rosemary.

Nutritional Information Per Serving:

Calories 210| Fat 10.1g |Sodium 325mg | Carbs 5g | Fibre 1.6g | Sugar 8g | Protein 25g

Dijon Salmon with Green Bean Pilaf

Ingredients:

- 1¼ pounds wild salmon, skinned and cut into 4 portions
- 3 tablespoons extra-virgin olive oil, divided
- 1 tablespoon minced garlic
- ¾ teaspoon salt
- 2 tablespoons mayonnaise
- 2 teaspoons whole-grain mustard
- ½ teaspoon ground pepper, divided
- 12 ounces thin green beans, cut into thirds
- 1 small lemon, zested and cut into 4 wedges
- 2 tablespoons pine nuts
- 1 (8-ounce) package precooked brown rice
- 2 tablespoons water
- chopped fresh parsley for garnish

Prep Time:	05 minutes
Cook Time:	25 minutes
Serves:	4

Preparation:

1. Preheat oven to 425°F. Line a rimmed baking sheet with foil or parchment paper.
2. Brush the salmon with 1 tablespoon of oil and place on the prepared baking sheet.
3. Crush the garlic and salt into a paste with the side of a chef's knife or fork. Mix a little less than a teaspoon of garlic paste in a small bowl with mayonnaise, mustard and ¼ teaspoon of pepper. Distribute the mixture over the fish.
4. With a fork, grill the salmon in the thickest part until it crumbles easily, 6 to 8 minutes per inch of thickness.
5. Meanwhile, heat the remaining 2 tablespoons of oil in a large skillet over medium heat. Add the green beans, lemon zest, pine nuts, remaining garlic paste and ¼ teaspoon of pepper; Cook, stirring constantly, until beans are tender, 2 to 4 minutes. Reduce the heat to medium.
6. Add the rice and water and cook, stirring constantly, 2 to 3 minutes, until heated through.
7. Sprinkle the salmon with parsley if you wish and serve with the green bean pilaf and lemon wedges.

Serving Suggestion: Serve the Dijon Salmon with Green Bean Pilaf with salad

Variation Tip: Walnuts or pecans in case not having pine nuts.

Nutritional Information Per Serving:

Calories 442| Fat 24.1g |Sodium 605mg | Carbs 21.5g | Fibre 3.6g | Sugar 1.8g | Protein 32.5g

Soups and Salad

Broccoli Cheese Soup

Ingredients:

- 1 head cauliflower, removed from thick stalk and cut into small pieces
- organic vegetable stock
- 1 head broccoli, removed from thick stalk, cut into small bite size pieces
- 2 organic carrots, sliced
- 1 can organic northern white beans
- ¾ cup coconut milk, unsweetened and divided
- ½ cup nutritional yeast
- 1 teaspoon garlic powder
- 1 to 2 teaspoon salt
- ½ teaspoon thyme, optional
- black pepper to taste, optional

Prep Time:	10 minutes
Cook Time:	25 minutes
Serves:	4

Preparation:

1. Place ½ can of vegetable and cauliflower broth in a large saucepan. Cover and cook, 12 to 15 minutes or until the cauliflower is tender.
2. While the cauliflower is cooking, chop the broccoli and chop the carrots.
3. Once the cauliflower is tender, use a hand blender to mix the cauliflower in the pot (or put it in the blender and blend in portions, being careful of hot liquids).
4. Add the remaining vegetable broth, broccoli, carrots, garlic powder, salt and thyme to the cauliflower puree. Stir and cover for 7 minutes or until broccoli is tender.
5. While the soup is cooking, rinse and drain the can of Northern white beans. Stir with ½ cup of coconut milk until smooth.
6. Once the broccoli is tender, add beans and ¼ cup of extra coconut milk to the soup.
7. Add ½ cup of nutritional yeast and stir to combine.
8. Let cool a little before tasting.

Serving Suggestion: Serve the Broccoli Cheese Soup with chips.

Variation Tip: Use almond milk in case not having coconut milk.

Nutritional Information Per Serving:

Calories 102| Fat 1g |Sodium 605mg | Carbs 15g | Fibre 6g | Sugar 4g | Protein 8g

Curried Coconut Pumpkin Soup

Ingredients:

- 1 tablespoon coconut oil
- 1 yellow onion, diced
- 2 cloves garlic, minced
- 1 teaspoon minced ginger
- 1 teaspoon curry powder
- 1 (15-ounce) can pumpkin purée
- 2 cups vegetable broth
- 1 (14-ounce) can coconut milk
- optional garnishes: extra coconut milk, pumpkin seeds

Prep Time:	05 minutes
Cook Time:	15 minutes
Serves:	6

Preparation:

1. In a large saucepan, heat the oil over medium heat. Add the onion and sauté for 4 minutes until just tender.
2. Add the garlic, ginger and curry powder and cook for 1 minute until fragrant.
3. Add the pumpkin puree, broth and coconut milk. Increase the heat to high and bring to a boil.
4. Reduce the heat to a minimum. Cover and simmer for about 10 minutes.
5. Remove the stove. Use a hand blender to puree the soup smooth. Alternatively, put in a traditional blender and puree in portions until you get a smooth mixture.
6. Season to taste with salt and pepper. Serve hot, topped with a dash of coconut milk and pumpkin seeds, if using.

Serving Suggestion: Serve the Curried Coconut Pumpkin Soup with potato chips.

Variation Tip: Use soy milk in case not having coconut milk.

Nutritional Information Per Serving:

Calories 182| Fat 17g |Sodium 305mg | Carbs 10.5g | Fibre 3g | Sugar 4g | Protein 2g

Asparagus Soup

Ingredients:

- 2 small boiling potatoes
- ¼ cup fat-free sour cream
- 1 pound asparagus
- vegetable broth
- 2 tablespoons olive oil
- 1 cup chopped onion
- 2 cloves garlic, crushed
- 1 (8-ounce) package sliced fresh mushrooms
- 1 clove garlic, crushed
- ¼ cup dry white wine (Optional)
- 1 pinch cayenne pepper
- salt and ground black pepper to taste

Prep Time:	15 minutes
Cook Time:	40 minutes
Serves:	6

Preparation:

1. Put the potatoes in a small saucepan with enough water to cover them; Bring to a boil, then reduce the heat to medium-low, cover the pot and simmer for about 20 minutes until tender.
2. Drain the potatoes and put them in a bowl; add sour cream and mix gently; scrape into the bowl of a blender.
3. Cut the asparagus into 3 parts: woody tips, tips and central pieces.
4. Combine the woody tips of the asparagus with the vegetable broth in a saucepan; Bring to a boil and cook until woody ends are tender. Remove the woody ends with a skimmer and discard them.
5. Put 2 tablespoons of broth with the asparagus tips in a bowl. Put the rest of the broth in the blender with the potatoes.
6. Chop the middle asparagus quarters.
7. Heat olive oil in a pan over low heat; Boil and stir the chopped asparagus, chopped onion and 2 crushed garlic cloves in hot oil until asparagus is tender, about 10 minutes. Add to the broth in the blender, collect the oil in the saucepan.
8. Combine mixture in blender over high heat until smooth and creamy. Return to the pot.
9. Cook the sliced mushrooms and 1 crushed garlic clove in the remaining oil over medium heat and stir until the mushrooms are tender, 3 to 5 minutes. Add the white wine; Cook for another 1 to 2 minutes. Add the mushroom mixture to the soup.
10. Heat the asparagus tips and broth in the microwave for 2 minutes. Stir into the soup.
11. Season the soup with cayenne pepper, salt and black pepper.

Serving Suggestion: Serve the Asparagus Soup with garlic bread.

Variation Tip: Use coconut cream in case not having sour cream.

Nutritional Information Per Serving:

Calories 167| Fat 24.1g |Sodium 485mg | Carbs 22.5g | Fibre 4.6g | Sugar 7.8g | Protein 5g

Chicken Pot Pie Soup

Ingredients:

- 2 tablespoons ghee
- 1 medium onion, peeled and diced
- 2 medium carrots, peeled and diced
- 2 celery stalks, diced
- cloves garlic, peeled and minced
- 2 ounces button or baby bella mushrooms, diced
- ⅓ cup coconut flour
- 2 cups organic chicken stock
- 3 cups shredded cooked chicken
- 1 pound Yukon gold potatoes, peeled & diced
- 1 cup chopped asparagus
- 1 teaspoon Italian seasoning (check labels!)
- ½ teaspoon salt
- ½ teaspoon freshly-cracked black pepper
- ½ cup raw cashews

Prep Time:	05 minutes
Cook Time:	30 minutes
Serves:	4

Preparation:

1. Put the water and cashews in a bowl and let soak for an hour. After soaking, put the cashews and water in a blender or food processor and stir until smooth. Pass the mixture through a sieve and discard the cashew pulp. Store the cashew milk.
2. In a large saucepan, heat the ghee over medium heat until melted. Add the onion, carrots and celery. Sauté for 6 to 7 minutes, stirring frequently, until onion is tender and translucent. Add the garlic and mushrooms and sauté for another 2 to 3 minutes, stirring frequently, until the garlic is fragrant.
3. Add coconut flour until completely combined and sauté for an additional minute, stirring occasionally. Gradually add the chicken broth and cashew milk, stirring frequently. Add the chicken, potatoes, asparagus, Italian seasoning, salt and pepper until combined.
4. Bring the mixture to a boil (be careful not to boil!), Stirring occasionally. Then reduce the heat to medium-low and simmer the soup for 15 to 20 minutes until the potatoes are tender and cooked through.
5. Season the soup to taste and, if necessary, season with additional salt and pepper.

Serving Suggestion: Serve the Chicken Pot Pie Soup with toast.

Variation Tip: Almond in case not having cashew.

Nutritional Information Per Serving:

Calories 485| Fat 12.1g |Sodium 905mg | Carbs 56g | Fibre 13.6g | Sugar 11.8g | Protein 39.5g

Sweet Potato and Arugula Salad

Ingredients:

- 6 cups ½-inch-diced sweet potatoes (4 to 6 large sweet potatoes)
- 1 tablespoon extra-virgin olive oil
- kosher salt and freshly ground black pepper
- 2 cups loosely packed baby arugula
- scallions, white and light green parts only, thinly sliced
- ¼ cup mayonnaise
- 2 tablespoons fresh lemon juice
- 2 tablespoons grated Parmesan

Prep Time:	15 minutes
Cook Time:	45 minutes
Serves:	8

Preparation:

1. Preheat oven to 400°F.
2. Spray a baking sheet with non-stick cooking spray.
3. In a large bowl, toss the sweet potatoes with the olive oil, ½ teaspoon of salt and ¼ teaspoon of pepper. Place on prepared baking sheet and bake for 20 minutes. Stir the potatoes and cook for another 15 to 20 minutes until tender. Let cool completely.
4. In a large bowl, combine the cooled sweet potatoes, arugula and chives.
5. In a small bowl, whisk together mayonnaise, lemon juice and Parmesan. Season with salt and pepper.
6. Just before serving, brush the dressing with the sweet potato and arugula mixture.

Serving Suggestion: Serve the Sweet Potato and Arugula Salad with grilled chicken.

Variation Tip: Use kale or spinach in case not having baby arugula.

Nutritional Information Per Serving:

Calories 442| Fat 24.1g |Sodium 605mg | Carbs 21.5g | Fibre 3.6g | Sugar 1.8g | Protein 32.5g

Kale Apple and Quinoa Salad

Ingredients:

Salad

- ½ cup tricolour dry quinoa
- cups slightly packed chopped kale
- 2 crisp sweet apples, cored and chopped
- 1 cup walnuts, lightly toasted and roughly chopped
- ½ cup dried cranberries
- 4 ounces goat cheese, crumbled

Dressing

- ½ cup olive oil
- ¼ cup fresh lemon juice
- 2 tablespoons honey
- 1½ teaspoons Dijon mustard
- salt to taste

Preparation:

1. Cook quinoa and cool: Cook quinoa according to directions on package and cool completely.
2. Whisk dressing ingredients: While quinoa is cooling, whisk together olive oil, lemon juice, honey, Dijon and salt in a jar or bowl.
3. Pour ¾ dressing over kale, chill: Add kale to a salad bowl, whisk dressing once more then pour ¾ of the dressing over kale and toss until kale is evenly coated. Cover bowl and chill 15 minutes (adding the dressing and letting it rest helps soften kale a bit).
4. Toss in remaining mix-ins and dressing: Remove salad from refrigerator, add apples, quinoa, walnuts and cranberries. For remaining dressing over salad then toss. Add goat cheese and toss just lightly.
5. Serve or store covered in refrigerator for up to 4 hours

Prep Time:	20 minutes
Cook Time:	15 minutes
Serves:	6

Serving Suggestion: Serve the Kale Apple and Quinoa Salad with carnitas.

Variation Tip: Use barley in case not having quinoa.

Nutritional Information Per Serving:

Calories 388| Fat 27g |Sodium 95mg | Carbs 31.5g | Fibre 3g | Sugar 18g | Protein 5g

Strawberry Spinach Salad with Chicken and Avocado

Ingredients:

Dressing:

- ¼ cup extra virgin olive oil
- 1 tablespoon golden balsamic vinegar
- 1 teaspoon sugar
- 1 tablespoon roughly chopped fresh tarragon
- ¼ teaspoon kosher salt
- ¼ teaspoon freshly ground black pepper

Salad:

- 2 boneless skinless chicken breasts
- 2 cups loosely packed fresh spinach
- 6 to 8 large strawberries, hulled and quartered
- 1 avocado, peeled, seeded and cut into chunks
- 3 to 4 thinly sliced rings of red onion
- ¼ cup feta cheese
- 2 tablespoons sliced almonds

Prep Time:	05 minutes
Cook Time:	30 minutes
Serves:	2

Preparation:

1. Whisk extra virgin olive oil with balsamic vinegar, sugar, tarragon, kosher salt and freshly ground black pepper in a small bowl.
2. Place the chicken breasts in a shallow bowl and cover with half the dressing, cover and refrigerate for 30 minutes to 2 hours.
3. Spray a 12-inch grill pan or non-stick skillet with cooking spray and heat over medium-high heat.
4. Place the chicken breast on the hot grill. Sauté for 3 minutes then flip the chicken breast. Cook for another 3 minutes and turn.
5. Reduce the cooking temperature to medium-low and cook the chicken for another 20 to 25 minutes, turning every 5 minutes. The cooking time depends on the thickness of the chicken, but is over when it reaches an internal temperature of 165°F or 73°C. Let the chicken rest for 5 minutes, then cut into ¼-inch slices.
6. Place the spinach, strawberries and red onion in a bowl. Toss lightly with the rest of the dressing.
7. Add avocado and chicken slices and garnish with feta cheese and almond slices.
8. Use immediately.

Serving Suggestion: Serve the Strawberry Spinach Salad with Chicken and Avocado with roasted turkey.

Variation Tip: Use honey instead of sugar.

Nutritional Information Per Serving:

Calories 759| Fat 54g |Sodium 705mg | Carbs 35g | Fibre 16g | Sugar 18g | Protein 35g

Cucumber Salad

Ingredients:

- 1 teaspoon salt
- 1 cup white vinegar
- 1½ cups sugar
- 1 teaspoon celery seed
- ¼ cup vegetable oil
- 5 cups cucumber slices
- 1 medium sweet onion, thinly sliced into rings
- 1 large yellow bell pepper, thinly sliced

Preparation:

1. In a medium saucepan, bring the salt, vinegar, sugar, celery seeds and vegetable oil to a boil, then remove the saucepan from the heat and let cool.

Prep Time:	20 minutes
Cook Time:	00 minutes
Serves:	4

2. In a large bowl, combine the sliced cucumbers, onions and peppers with the liquid mixture and place in the refrigerator for at least 2 hours and overnight. Serve cold.

Serving Suggestion: Serve the Cucumber Salad with grilled chicken.

Variation Tip: Use apple cider vinegar in case not having white vinegar.

Nutritional Information Per Serving:

Calories 442| Fat 24.1g |Sodium 605mg | Carbs 21.5g | Fibre 3.6g | Sugar 1.8g | Protein 32.5g

Snack and Side Recipes

Grain Free Rosemary Crackers

Ingredients:

- 1 cup almond flour
- ¾ cup tapioca flour/starch
- ½ teaspoon. sea salt
- 1 tablespoon. coconut oil, in liquid state
- 1 large egg
- 1 teaspoon dried rosemary
- ¼ cup nutritional yeast
- water, kept in a cup that you can measure out by the 1 tablespoon full.

Preparation:

1. Combine all ingredients except water in a bowl. Knead well.
2. When the dough seems to crumble, add 1 tablespoon of water. Knead well between additions at the same time.
3. If you end up adding too much water, just add a little more tapioca flour (about ½ teaspoon at a time).
4. Roll the dough between two pieces of parchment paper until the dough is about ⅛-inch-thick.
5. Cut them into squares and transfer them to a baking sheet with a spatula. Pricking the cookies with a fork is optional and takes a bit of time, but I found them crispier when I made this.
6. Bake at 325°F for about 20 to 30 minutes. They will be heavy (won't burn!) And will have a slightly golden tint when cooked.
7. Let cool completely before eating, otherwise they won't become crispy.

Prep Time:	30 minutes
Cook Time:	30 minutes
Serves:	55

Serving Suggestion: Serve the Grain Free Rosemary Crackers with tea/coffee.

Variation Tip: Use coconut flour in case not having almond flour.

Nutritional Information Per Serving:

Calories 22| Fat 1g |Sodium 15mg | Carbs 2g | Fibre 3.6g | Sugar 1.8g | Protein 2.5g

Tuna Pinwheels

Ingredients:

- 1 standard-sized whole grain tortilla
- a 6-ounce can water-packed tuna
- 2 tablespoons clean mayo

Preparation:

1. Combine the tuna and mayonnaise in a small bowl.
2. Once everything is well mixed, spread the tuna over the tortilla.
3. Roll up the tortilla like a mat and cut it into slices ½ to ¾ inch wide.
4. Wrap in a food grade container and keep with a cold compress until noon. Enjoy!

Serving Suggestion: Serve the Tuna Pinwheels with tea.

Variation Tip: Use salmon in case not having tuna.

Nutritional Information Per Serving:

Calories 420| Fat 24g |Sodium 835mg | Carbs 21.5g | Fibre 3.6g | Sugar 1.8g | Protein 35g

Prep Time:	10 minutes
Cook Time:	00 minutes
Serves:	1

Doritos

Ingredients:

- 1 package clean, corn tortillas
- ½ cup nutritional yeast
- 1 tablespoon garlic powder
- 1 teaspoon onion powder
- oil in an oil sprayer

Preparation:

1. Cut the tortillas into chips and lay them out on baking sheets lined with parchment paper.
2. Spray on an oil spray, making sure to cover the tops of the chips as evenly as possible.
3. In a bowl, combine the nutritional yeast, garlic powder and onion powder.
4. Sprinkle the yeast mixture over the fries.
5. Bake at 325°F for 20 to 30 minutes. This time may vary depending on the oven, so set your timer for 15 minutes, then check every 5 minutes thereafter. They go from finished to burnt quite quickly. So watch them carefully. Also, do not cook them until they are completely crispy. They'll get tough as they cool, and if you cook them crispy, you'll look more like a jawbreaker once they cool.
6. Take out of the oven and let cool completely.

Prep Time:	10 minutes
Cook Time:	20 minutes
Serves:	4

Serving Suggestion: Serve the Doritos with salsa.

Variation Tip: Use gluten free tortillas instead of corn tortillas.

Nutritional Information Per Serving:

Calories 442| Fat 24.1g |Sodium 605mg | Carbs 21.5g | Fibre 3.6g | Sugar 1.8g | Protein 32.5g

Roasted Curried Chickpeas

Ingredients:

- 1 (15-ounce) can chickpeas, drained and rinsed, no sugar added or 1⅓ cups homemade, plain chickpeas
- 1 teaspoon curry powder
- 1 teaspoon Garam masala
- 1 teaspoon garlic powder
- 1 tablespoon olive oil
- salt to taste

Preparation:

1. In a medium bowl, combine all the ingredients together and toss well to cover the chickpeas with the spices.
2. Pour them onto an ungreased baking sheet and spread as much of the mash as possible in a single layer.
3. Cook over low and slow heat at 300°F for about 1 hour or until golden brown and crisp.
4. Let cool completely and store in an airtight container in the refrigerator for up to 3 weeks.

Prep Time:	20 minutes
Cook Time:	1 minutes
Serves:	4

Serving Suggestion: Serve the Roasted Curried Chickpeas with coffee.

Variation Tip: Use fresh garlic case not having garlic powder.

Nutritional Information Per Serving:

Calories 177| Fat 5g |Sodium 399mg | Carbs 27.5g | Fibre 5.6g | Sugar 0.8g | Protein 5.2g

Baked Garlic Parmesan Potato Wedges

Ingredients:

- 3 to 4 large russet potatoes, sliced into wedges
- 2 tablespoons olive oil
- 1 teaspoon salt
- 2 teaspoons garlic powder
- 2 teaspoons Italian seasoning
- ½ cup shredded parmesan cheese
- optional: fresh parsley (or cilantro), ranch or blue cheese dressing for dipping

Preparation:

Prep Time:	15 minutes
Cook Time:	35 minutes
Serves:	4

1. Preheat the oven to 375°F. Lightly grease a large baking sheet and set aside.
2. Place the potato slices in a large bowl. Drizzle with olive oil and turn to coat. Combine salt, garlic powder and Italian spices in a small bowl. Sprinkle the potato wedges with the grated cheese, toss to brush, then sprinkle with the spice blend.
3. Place the potato slices skin-side down in a single layer on the prepared baking sheet. Bake for 25 to 35 minutes, until the potatoes are tender and golden yellow. To soak, sprinkle with freshly chopped parsley and dressing.

Serving Suggestion: Serve the Baked Garlic Parmesan Potato Wedges with sauce.

Variation Tip: Use sweet potatoes in case not having potatoes.

Nutritional Information Per Serving:

Calories 404| Fat 24.1g |Sodium 1305mg | Carbs 52g | Fibre 4g | Sugar 2g | Protein 15g

Garlic Butter Quinoa

Ingredients:

- 1 cup quinoa
- 1 tablespoon vegan butter or butter/ghee
- 2 to 3 teaspoons simply organic garlic powder
- ½ teaspoon sea salt
- 2 cups vegetable broth

Preparation:

1. Put all the ingredients in a small saucepan. Bring to a boil and stir until the butter is melted.
2. Cover and reduce to low heat and simmer for 15 minutes. Remove the lid, remove it from the heat and loosen it with a fork.
3. Let steep for 5 minutes then serve.

Serving Suggestion: Serve the Garlic Butter Quinoa with salad.

Variation Tip: Use barley in case not having quinoa.

Nutritional Information Per Serving:

Calories 190| Fat 4.1g |Sodium 705mg | Carbs 30g | Fibre 3g | Sugar 1g | Protein 5g

Prep Time:	05 minutes
Cook Time:	15 minutes
Serves:	4

Easy Roasted Baby Bok Choy

Ingredients:

- 1 pound bok choy
- ¼ cup olive oil
- pepper to taste
- 2 tablespoons low-sodium soy sauce
- 1 tablespoon lemon juice
- ½ teaspoon garlic powder
- red pepper flakes to taste

Preparation:

1. Preheat the oven to 450°F. Slide the rack into the middle of the oven. Line a large baking sheet with parchment paper.
2. Cut the baby bok choy in half lengthwise and cut off the dry ends (the white part) if necessary.
3. Place the baby bok choy on the baking sheet. For the olive oil, grind a little pepper on both sides of each piece of bok choy (and rub it). I prefer to grill it upside down first.
4. Place the baking sheet in the oven and grill for 5 minutes on each side (it will become tender and crisp with a few crispy leaves). If you want more, roast it a bit more.
5. Meanwhile, combine soy sauce, lemon juice, garlic powder and red pepper flakes in a small bowl.
6. Once the baby bok choy is cooked to your liking, drizzle each piece with the sauce. Use immediately.

Prep Time:	05 minutes
Cook Time:	10 minutes
Serves:	4

Serving Suggestion: Serve the Easy Roasted Baby Bok Choy with grilled chicken.

Variation Tip: Use coconut aminos in case not having soy sauce

Nutritional Information Per Serving:

Calories 144| Fat 14.1g |Sodium 305mg | Carbs 32g | Fibre 3.6g | Sugar 1.8g | Protein 2.5g

Deviled Eggs

Ingredients:

- 10 large hard boiled eggs (shelled)
- ½ cup mayonnaise
- 1 pinch paprika

Preparation:

1. Peel and cut the hard-boiled eggs in half, place the yolks in a separate bowl.
2. Put the whites in a fountain and set aside.
3. Add the mayonnaise to the egg yolk and stir until smooth. You can use a blender for this if you want, I just use a fork. The amount of mayonnaise you use depends on how creamy you want the mixture to be. Adjust the amount to your liking.

Prep Time:	20 minutes
Cook Time:	15 minutes
Serves:	4

4. Place the yolks in a zippered plastic sandwich bag and cut out a corner.
5. Holding the bag like an ice pack, sprinkle the egg yolk in the egg white and distribute it evenly.
6. Sprinkle the eggs over the eggs with a light pinch of paprika.
7. Store in the refrigerator covered with plastic wrap until ready to serve.

Serving Suggestion: Serve the Deviled Eggs with salad.

Variation Tip: Use Greek yogurt in case not having mayonnaises.

Nutritional Information Per Serving:

Calories 72| Fat 6g |Sodium 65mg | Carbs 21.5g | Fibre 3.6g | Sugar 1.8g | Protein 3g

Vegetarian Recipes

Lentils and Rice

Ingredients:

- ½ cup finely chopped red onion
- ½ cup finely chopped red bell pepper
- ½ cup finely chopped white mushrooms
- 1 tablespoon oil
- 1 tablespoon garlic powder
- 1 teaspoon ground cumin
- 1 teaspoon curry powder
- 1 cup brown lentils (dry)
- 1½ cups brown basmati rice
- ½ cup vegetable broth

Preparation:

Prep Time:	15 minutes
Cook Time:	25 minutes
Serves:	4

1. Heat the oil in a saucepan add onion, pepper and mushrooms, sauté the vegetable.
2. Sauté the vegetables until the onions are translucent, then add the spices and stir again.
3. Add the lentils and rice and toss well to coat the rice with spices.
4. Rice and lentils with the spices and vegetables of this.
5. Finally add the broth and mix well. Cover the sauce pan in lid and cook the rice and lentil until cooked about 20 minutes.
6. Salt as needed and serve.

Serving Suggestion: Serve the Lentils and Rice with salad.

Variation Tip: Use quinoa in case not having rice.

Nutritional Information Per Serving:

Calories 312| Fat 6g |Sodium 465mg | Carbs 53g | Fibre 16g | Sugar 3g | Protein 11g

Chickpea Tacos

Ingredients:

- 2 tablespoons oil
- ½ cup cooked chickpeas
- 1 tablespoon garlic powder
- 1 tablespoon onion powder
- 1 tablespoon chili powder
- 1 tablespoon ground cumin
- taco toppings
- tortillas

Preparation:

1. Combine oil, chickpeas and spices in a large skillet and sauté until beans are heated through and well coated with spices.
2. When the mixture is completely hot and everything is combined, use it to make your tacos in place of meat.

Prep Time:	05 minutes
Cook Time:	15 minutes
Serves:	4

Serving Suggestion: Serve the Chickpea Tacos with salad.

Variation Tip: Use fresh garlic and onion in case not having dried garlic and onion.

Nutritional Information Per Serving:

Calories 272| Fat 16g |Sodium 65mg | Carbs 35g | Fibre 10g | Sugar 8g | Protein 13g

Butternut Squash Risotto

Ingredients:

- 1 cup vegetable broth
- 4 cups cooked brown rice
- 2 tablespoons garlic powder
- 1 teaspoon salt
- 2 teaspoons ground nutmeg
- 2 teaspoons ground sage
- 2 cups butternut squash puree
- 4 ounces sliced mushrooms
- 4 ounces grated mozzarella cheese
- ¼ cup grated parmesan cheese
- ¼ cup fresh parsley
- salt and pepper to taste

Prep Time:	05 minutes
Cook Time:	15 minutes
Serves:	4

Preparation:

1. I mashed a whole pumpkin by cutting it in half, removing the seeds, and baking it, side down on a baking sheet with about ½ inch of water in the pot, until it is smooth and easily pierced with a knife. Then I mixed it gently. But you can also buy butter and nut mash if you prefer or replace it with pumpkin mash.
2. Heat the vegetable broth in a large skillet or wok.
3. Add parboiled rice (if using) or cauliflower with rice.
4. Add all the spices and the walnut puree as well as the mushrooms.
5. When the broth is a bit cooked and the mushrooms appear cooked, add the cheese and stir until melted.
6. Once the cheese has melted in the sauce, remove the pan from the heat and add the fresh parsley, reserving something for the garnish if desired.
7. Season to taste with salt and pepper.

Serving Suggestion: Serve the Butternut Squash Risotto with salad

Variation Tip: Use cooked quinoa in case not having cooked brown rice

Nutritional Information Per Serving:

Calories 239| Fat 6g |Sodium 65mg | Carbs 35g | Fibre 4g | Sugar 1.8g | Protein 9g

Sweet Potato Curry

Ingredients:

- 2 cups peeled, diced sweet potatoes (no larger than ½ inch pieces)
- 1½ cups sliced carrots
- 27 ounces canned coconut milk
- a 28-ounce can tomatoes, diced
- 1 tablespoon ground cumin
- 2 tablespoon curry powder
- 1 tablespoon Garam Masala
- 1½ cups dry red lentils
- 4 cups vegetable broth or chicken broth, if you prefer
- 2 tablespoons garlic powder
- 2 tablespoons onion powder
- 4 cups raw spinach leaves, chopped
- salt to taste at serving

Prep Time:	20 minutes
Cook Time:	8 hours
Serves:	14

Preparation:

1. Put all the ingredients (except the raw spinach) in the slow cooker and stir well.
2. Reduce the heat and cook for 7 to 8 hours or until the sweet potatoes and lentils are tender and cooked through.
3. After cooking, add the raw spinach until just tender.
4. Season with salt and serve.

Serving Suggestion: Serve the Sweet Potato Curry with cauliflower rice.

Variation Tip: Use almond milk in case not having coconut milk.

Nutritional Information Per Serving:

Calories 309| Fat 16g |Sodium 465mg | Carbs 40g | Fibre 13g | Sugar 8g | Protein 9g

Sautéed Zucchini with Mint, Basil & Pine Nuts

Ingredients:

- 1 pound zucchini (or any summer squash), sliced into ½-inch rounds
- 3 tablespoons (or less) olive oil, divided
- 3 small cloves garlic
- 10 or more mint leaves
- 5 or more basil leaves
- 1 heaping tablespoon capers, rinsed
- 2 tablespoons pine nuts or walnuts, lightly toasted
- 1 to 2 teaspoon red wine vinegar
- sea salt and freshly ground pepper, to taste
- additional mint and basil, torn, to garnish

Preparation:

1. Heat 1 tablespoon of olive oil in a 10-inch skillet over medium heat.
2. When the oil is hot, add half the zucchini and sauté every few minutes until golden, about 15 minutes. Do not salt them right away!
3. While the zucchini is cooking, chop the garlic, mint, basil and capers so that they mix and become a kind of pesto with a knife.
4. When the zucchini is golden, remove them from the pan and cook the rest of the zucchini in another tablespoon of oil, as you did with the first batch.
5. Note: I cut the oil here, but if you need a little more frying, give it a try. Then return the first batch to the pot, along with the garlic and herb mixture and vinegar to taste. Taste with salt, add a good pinch, plus a few peppercorns. Mix well. Add the nuts. Turn everything out onto a plate. Sprinkle more herbs just before serving, if using

Prep Time:	15 minutes
Cook Time:	15 minutes
Serves:	4

Serving Suggestion: Serve the Sautéed Zucchini with Mint, Basil & Pine Nuts with garlic bread.

Variation Tip: Use white balsamic in case not having red wine vinegar.

Nutritional Information Per Serving:

Calories 72| Fat 6g |Sodium 65mg | Carbs 21.5g | Fibre 3.6g | Sugar 1.8g | Protein 3g

Red Cabbage Pasta

Ingredients:

- ½ pound pasta
- 4 cups shredded kale
- 4 cups shredded red cabbage
- 1 cup chopped red onion
- 1 tablespoon coconut oil
- 1 tablespoon tamari
- 2 teaspoons garlic powder
- peanut sauce, to taste
- vegetable broth

Preparation:

1. Bring the pasta to a boil.
2. While the pasta cooks, add the kale, red cabbage, onion and oil to a large skillet.
3. Fry until the onions are translucent and the cabbage and kale have collapsed.
4. Add the tamari and garlic powder, mix well and set aside. Only use vegetable broth if there is no more oil and you need to continue cooking.
5. If you haven't made your peanut sauce yet, do so now.
6. When all three components are ready, mix everything together and serve.
7. Sprinkle chopped peanuts on top for a nice, added texture.

Prep Time:	10 minutes
Cook Time:	30 minutes
Serves:	4

Serving Suggestion: Serve the Red Cabbage Pasta with salad.

Variation Tip: Use spinach in case not having kale.

Nutritional Information Per Serving:

Calories 302| Fat 6g |Sodium 265mg | Carbs 56g | Fibre 3.6g | Sugar 1.8g | Protein 11g

Chickpea Basil Quinoa Salad

Ingredients:

- 3 cups cooked quinoa (cooked with vegetable broth to package directions)
- 1 cup cooked chickpeas (if canned, drain and rinse)
- ½ cup finely chopped basil
- 2 tablespoons balsamic vinegar
- salt to taste

Preparation:

1. Combine all ingredients together in a large mixing bowl and toss to combine.
2. Serve as a main meal or tasty side dish.

Serving Suggestion: Serve the Chickpea Basil Quinoa Salad with garlic bread.

Prep Time:	10 minutes
Cook Time:	00 minutes
Serves:	4

Variation Tip: Use cooked barley in case not having cooked quinoa.

Nutritional Information Per Serving:

Calories 240 | Fat 6g | Sodium 15mg | Carbs 45g | Fibre 6g | Sugar 4g | Protein 9g

Corn Casserole

Ingredients:

- ½ cup butter (melted and cooled. I used vegan butter)
- ⅔ cup whole grain spelt flour + 2 tablespoon.
- ¼ cup cornmeal
- 3 tablespoons coconut sugar
- 1 batch creamed corn (see recipe link above)
- salt to taste

Preparation:

1. Preheat the oven to 350°F.
2. Stir in the additional 2 tablespoons. Beat flour in melted butter until smooth.
3. Combine the cream of corn and all the ingredients (including the butter / flour mixture) in a large mixing bowl.
4. Mix well to combine.
5. Pour the dough in a greased baking dish.
6. Bake for 1 hour or until cooked through.
7. Let cool a bit and serve.

Prep Time:	20 minutes
Cook Time:	60 minutes
Serves:	4

Serving Suggestion: Serve the Corn Casserole with salad.

Variation Tip: Use maple syrup in case not having coconut sugar.

Nutritional Information Per Serving:

Calories 372| Fat 6g |Sodium 765mg | Carbs 59g | Fibre 3g | Sugar 18g | Protein 6g

Lentil Sloppy Joes

Ingredients:

- 2 teaspoons olive oil
- 1 medium yellow onion diced
- 1 green pepper diced
- 3 cloves garlic minced
- 3 cup cooked lentils
- 2 tablespoons chili powder
- 2 teaspoons oregano
- a pinch of cayenne pepper
- 2 cups crushed tomatoes
- ¼ cup tomato paste
- 3 tablespoons maple syrup
- 2 tablespoons yellow mustard
- whole grain burger buns

Prep Time:	20 minutes
Cook Time:	10 minutes
Serves:	8

Preparation:

1. Heat the oil in a large non-stick skillet over medium heat.
2. Add onion and peppers and sauté for about eight minutes or until just tender.
3. Add the garlic and sauté a few more minutes.
4. Add the cooked lentils, chili powder, oregano and cayenne pepper. Salt and pepper then add the tomato sauce and the tomato paste. Cook for another ten minutes (if it looks a bit dry or you just want it to be stickier, add a few more tomatoes and / or a few dashes of water).
5. Add the maple syrup and mustard and cook for about two more minutes.
6. Pour a cup of the sloppy joes filling over a whole grain burger bun. Enjoy!!

Serving Suggestion: Serve the Lentil Sloppy Joes with salad.

Variation Tip: Use honey in case not having maple syrup.

Nutritional Information Per Serving:

Calories 219| Fat 6g |Sodium 565mg | Carbs 35g | Fibre 13g | Sugar 11g | Protein 11g

Dessert Recipes

Carrot Cake

Ingredients:

- 1 20-ounce can pineapple, crushed
- 2 cups whole-wheat pastry flour,
- 2 teaspoons baking soda
- ½ teaspoon salt
- 2 teaspoons ground cinnamon
- 3 large eggs
- 1½ cups granulated sugar
- ¾ cup non-fat buttermilk,
- ½ cup canola oil
- 1 teaspoon vanilla extract
- 2 cups grated carrots
- ¼ cup unsweetened flaked coconut
- ½ cup chopped walnuts, toasted

Prep Time:	20 minutes
Cook Time:	45 minutes
Serves:	4

Preparation:

1. Preheat oven to 350°F. Spray a 9-inch-by-13-inch baking dish with cooking spray.
2. Drain the pineapple in a colander over a bowl and squeeze out the solids. Reserve the drained pineapple and ¼ cup of the juice.
3. In a medium bowl, combine flour, cinnamon, baking powder and salt. In a large bowl, whisk together the eggs, sugar, buttermilk, oil, vanilla and ¼ cup pineapple juice until combined.
4. Add the pineapple, carrots and ¼ cup of coconut. Add the dry ingredients and mix with a rubber spatula until just blended. Add the nuts. Scrape the dough into the prepared pan and distribute it evenly.
5. Bake cake until top springs back to touch and skewer inserted in centre comes out clean, 40 to 45 minutes. Let cool completely on a wire rack.

Serving Suggestion: Serve the Carrot Cake with chips.

Variation Tip: Use buttermilk powder in case not having butter milk.

Nutritional Information Per Serving:

Calories 341| Fat 6g |Sodium 565mg | Carbs 45g | Fibre 3g | Sugar 21g | Protein 6g

Peach & Blueberry Cobbler

Ingredients:

- 3 tablespoons unsalted butter
- 3 tablespoons canola oil
- 1 cup whole-wheat flour
- 1½ teaspoons baking powder
- ½ teaspoon salt
- 1 cup reduced-fat milk
- ½ cup sugar
- 1 teaspoon vanilla extract
- 3 ripe but firm peaches, (about 1 pound), pitted and sliced into eighths, or 3½ cups frozen
- 2 cups (1-pint) fresh or frozen blueberries

Prep Time:	20 minutes
Cook Time:	60 minutes
Serves:	4

Preparation:

1. Preheat the oven to 350°F.
2. Place butter and oil in a 12-inch cast iron skillet or 9-inch-by-13-inch baking sheet. Heat in the oven until melted and fragrant, 5 to 7 minutes.
3. Meanwhile, combine flour, baking powder and salt in a large bowl. Add the milk, sugar and vanilla; stir to combine.
4. Add the melted butter mixture to the dough and stir. For the dough in the hot pan. Spread the peaches and blueberries evenly over the dough.
5. Return pan to oven and bake until cobbler top is golden brown and dough is completely firm around fruit, 50 minutes to 1 hour. Place on a wire rack for at least 15 minutes to cool. Serve hot

Serving Suggestion: Serve the Peach & Blueberry Cobbler with chips.

Variation Tip: Use plant based milk in case not having reduced-fat milk.

Nutritional Information Per Serving:

Calories 196| Fat 6g |Sodium 565mg | Carbs 25g | Fibre 1.3g | Sugar 18g | Protein 3.1g

Strawberry Nice Cream

Ingredients:

- 1 pound fresh strawberries
- 2 medium bananas
- 1 tablespoon fresh lemon juice
- ¼ cup ice-cold water, as needed

Preparation:

1. Peel and roughly chop the strawberries. and the bananas.
2. Divide strawberries and bananas on separate sides of a baking sheet or on two platters. Freeze until firm, at least 12 hours.
3. Thaw strawberries at room temperature for 15 minutes. Transfer to a food processor; Pulse until finely chopped, about 10 pulses.
4. Add frozen bananas and lemon juice; Stir for 1 to 1½ minutes until smooth, adding up to ¼ cup of cold water if necessary to achieve desired consistency and scraping sides of bowl as needed.
5. Serve immediately or, for a firmer texture, transfer to a freezer-safe container and freeze for up to 30 minutes.

Prep Time:	20 minutes
Cook Time:	00 minutes
Serves:	4

Serving Suggestion: Serve the Strawberry Nice Cream with chips.

Variation Tip: Use any berries in case not having strawberries.

Nutritional Information Per Serving:

Calories 119| Fat 6g |Sodium 565mg | Carbs 25g | Fibre 1.3g | Sugar 12.1g | Protein 1.1g

Mango Fruit Leather

Ingredients:

- 3 large ripe mangoes, peeled and flesh cut away from the pit
- ½ cup water
- 1 teaspoon lemon juice

Preparation:

1. Preheat the oven to 200°F.
2. Line a large baking sheet with a rim of a non-stick baking mat.
3. Puree the mangoes, water and lemon juice in a blender until you get a smooth mass. Transfer to a medium saucepan and simmer over medium heat.
4. Reduce heat to simmer and cook, partially covered, until reduced to about 2 cups of mash, about 20 minutes.
5. Put the mash on the prepared baking sheet. Using a rubber spatula, spread very evenly into a thin rectangle no more than ⅛-inch-thick.
6. Bake for 4 to 6 hours until dry to the touch. Let cool completely.
7. Transfer the leather from the fruit to a piece of parchment paper (or waxed paper) about the same size.
8. Leave the parchment underneath and roll the closed skin of the fruit into a long cylinder. Cut into 2-cm-wide strips with a sharp knife or scissors.

Prep Time:	20 minutes
Cook Time:	4 to 6 hours
Serves:	4

Serving Suggestion: Serve the Mango Fruit Leather with snacks.

Variation Tip: Use any fruits in case not having mango.

Nutritional Information Per Serving:

Calories 89| Fat 6g |Sodium 565mg | Carbs 25g | Fibre 1.3g | Sugar 19.1g | Protein 1.1g

Dark Chocolate Frozen Banana Bites

Ingredients:

- 3 small (about 6-inch-long) ripe bananas, each cut into 6 (1-inch) slices
- 18 cocktail picks
- 5 ounces dark (85% cacao) chocolate, finely chopped
- 2 teaspoons coconut oil
- 2 tablespoons unsweetened shredded dried coconut, toasted
- 2 tablespoons chopped toasted almonds
- ½ teaspoon sea salt flakes

Preparation:

1. Pierce each banana slice with 1 cocktail stick and place them on a baking sheet lined with parchment paper. Freeze for 1 hour.
2. Pour water to a depth of 1 inch in the bottom of a double boiler over medium heat, bring to a gentle boil.
3. Reduce the heat to medium-low and let simmer. Place chocolate and oil in double boiler and cook, stirring frequently, until chocolate is melted and mixture is smooth, about 4 minutes.
4. Dip 1 slice of banana on a skewer in the chocolate mixture; Immediately sprinkle with a pinch of coconut and return to the baking sheet.
5. Repeat with the remaining coconut for 5 more banana slices, then with almonds for 6 banana slices, then with sea salt for the remaining 6 banana slices.
6. Freeze bites for 1 hour before serving.

Prep Time:	20 minutes
Cook Time:	05 minutes
Serves:	4

Serving Suggestion: Serve the Dark Chocolate Frozen Banana Bites with potatoes fries.

Variation Tip: Use walnuts in case not having almonds.

Nutritional Information Per Serving:

Calories 229| Fat 16g |Sodium 165mg | Carbs 25g | Fibre 5g | Sugar 11g | Protein 11g

Greek Yogurt with Warm Berry Sauce

Ingredients:

- ⅔ cup frozen blueberries
- ⅔ cup frozen blackberries
- ½ cup water
- ¼ cup sugar
- 2 tablespoons fresh lemon juice
- 1 tablespoon butter
- 2 cups plain 2% reduced-fat Greek yogurt

Preparation:

1. Combine the first 5 ingredients in a small saucepan. Bring the mixture to a boil.
2. Reduce the heat to medium-low. Simmer 10 minutes or until the sauce thickens. Add the butter.
3. Pour ½ cup of yogurt into each of 4 bowls; cover each serving with about ¼ cup of the sauce.

Serving Suggestion: Serve the Lentil Sloppy Joes with salad.

Prep Time:	20 minutes
Cook Time:	10 minutes
Serves:	4

Variation Tip: Use honey in case not having maple syrup.

Nutritional Information Per Serving:

Calories 119| Fat 5.6g |Sodium 65mg | Carbs 25g | Fibre 3g | Sugar 1g | Protein 12g

Tropical Fruit Pudding

Ingredients:

- 2 tablespoons maple syrup or other sweetener
- 24 ounces silken tofu
- 2 mangoes, peeled, pitted and cut into big chunks
- ½ teaspoon vanilla extract
- ⅛ teaspoon salt
- ¼ teaspoon coconut extract, optional
- ½ large pineapple, peeled, quartered and cored
- ¾ cup unsweetened shredded coconut

Preparation:

1. In a food processor or blender, add syrup, tofu, mangoes, vanilla, salt and coconut extract, if desired.
2. Puree and scrape sides of bowl as needed, until completely smooth, at least 1 minute. Transfer to a large bowl.
3. Cut the pineapple into ⅛-inch pieces and fold them into a pudding. Seal tightly and refrigerate for at least 30 minutes to several hours.
4. In a large skillet, cook the coconut over medium heat, stirring frequently for 5 to 10 minutes, until golden brown.
5. Take out of the pan and let cool. To serve, pour the pudding into bowls and sprinkle with toasted coconut.

Prep Time:	15 minutes
Cook Time:	10 minutes
Serves:	4

Serving Suggestion: Serve the Lentil Sloppy Joes with salad.

Variation Tip: Use honey in case not having maple syrup.

Nutritional Information Per Serving:

Calories 319| Fat 16g |Sodium 85mg | Carbs 53g | Fibre 7g | Sugar 11g | Protein 10g

4 Weeks Meal Plan

1st Week Meal Plan

Days	Breakfast	Lunch	Snacks	Dinner	Dessert
1	Breakfast Burritos	Almond-Crusted Chicken	Doritos	Garlic Lime Pork Chops	Carrot Cake
2	Loaded Veggie Avocado Quinoa Frittatas	Korean Beef	Roasted Curried Chickpeas	Tuna Burgers	Mango Fruit Leather
3	Pineapple Mango Smoothie	Broccoli Cheese Soup	Easy Roasted Baby Bok Choy	Chickpea Tacos	Tropical Fruit Pudding
4	Blueberry Quinoa Pancakes	Tuna Stuffed Avocado	Grain Free Rosemary Crackers	Chicken Fried Rice with Pineapple	Dark Chocolate Frozen Banana Bites
5	Banana Spinach Muffins	Pork Chops with Balsamic Peppers	Garlic Butter Quinoa	Meatball Spaghetti Squash Boats	Mango Fruit Leather
6	Fluffy Whole Wheat Zucchini Bread Pancakes	Dijon Salmon with Green Bean Pilaf	Tuna Pinwheels	Quinoa Fried Rice with Pork	Peach & Blueberry Cobbler
7	Whole Wheat Coconut Banana Waffles	Chicken Meatballs and Cauliflower Rice	Deviled Eggs	Beef-Stuffed Peppers	Strawberry Nice Cream

2nd Week Meal Plan

Days	Breakfast	Lunch	Snacks	Dinner	Dessert
1	Fluffy Whole Wheat Zucchini Bread Pancakes	Crispy Lemon Rosemary Brick Chicken	Tuna Pinwheels	Grilled Flank Steak with Mustardy Potato Salad	Tropical Fruit Pudding
2	Blueberry Quinoa Pancakes	Teriyaki Salmon Recipe	Deviled Eggs	Garlic Lime Pork Chops	Mango Fruit Leather
3	Delicious Immune Boosting Wellness Smoothie	Pesto Pasta with Ground Turkey	Baked Garlic Parmesan Potato Wedges	Brazilian Fish Stew	Carrot Cake
4	Loaded Veggie Avocado Quinoa Frittatas	Garlic Lime Flank Steak	Doritos	Asparagus Soup	Greek Yogurt with Warm Berry Sauce
5	Banana Spinach Muffins	Kale Apple and Quinoa Salad	Roasted Curried Chickpeas	Pork Chops with Balsamic Peppers	Dark Chocolate Frozen Banana Bites
6	Pineapple Mango Smoothie	Corn Casserole	Easy Roasted Baby Bok Choy	Pan Seared Salmon with Chia Seeds	Strawberry Nice Cream
7	Breakfast Burritos	One Pan Roasted Pork Tenderloin with Veggies	Grain Free Rosemary Crackers	Sticky Honey Garlic Chicken Wings	Peach & Blueberry Cobbler

3rd Week Meal Plan

Days	Breakfast	Lunch	Snacks	Dinner	Dessert
1	Delicious Immune Boosting Wellness Smoothie	Tuna Stuffed Avocado	Easy Roasted Baby Bok Choy	Curried Coconut Pumpkin Soup	Mango Fruit Leather
2	Blueberry Quinoa Pancakes	Meatball Spaghetti Squash Boats	Garlic Butter Quinoa	Broccoli Cheese Soup	Strawberry Nice Cream
3	Banana Spinach Muffins	Quinoa Fried Rice with Pork	Tuna Pinwheels	Sweet Potato and Arugula Salad	Tropical Fruit Pudding
4	Pineapple Mango Smoothie	Healthy Beef and Broccoli	Doritos	Kale Apple and Quinoa Salad	Peach & Blueberry Cobbler
5	Fluffy Whole Wheat Zucchini Bread Pancakes	Pesto Pasta with Ground Turkey	Deviled Eggs	Chicken Pot Pie Soup	Carrot Cake
6	Breakfast Burritos	Lemon and Basil Chicken Breasts	Grain Free Rosemary Crackers	Asparagus Soup	Greek Yogurt with Warm Berry Sauce
7	Loaded Veggie Avocado Quinoa Frittatas	Almond-Crusted Chicken	Roasted Curried Chickpeas	Strawberry Spinach Salad with Chicken and Avocado	Dark Chocolate Frozen Banana Bites

4th Week Meal Plan

Days	Breakfast	Lunch	Snacks	Dinner	Dessert
1	Breakfast Burritos	Grilled Flank Steak with Mustardy Potato Salad	Tuna Pinwheels	Tuna Stuffed Avocado	Dark Chocolate Frozen Banana Bites
2	Loaded Veggie Avocado Quinoa Frittatas	Garlic Lime Pork Chops	Deviled Eggs	Meatball Spaghetti Squash Boats	Mango Fruit Leather
3	Pineapple Mango Smoothie	Brazilian Fish Stew	Baked Garlic Parmesan Potato Wedges	Quinoa Fried Rice with Pork	Tropical Fruit Pudding
4	Blueberry Quinoa Pancakes	Asparagus Soup	Doritos	Healthy Beef and Broccoli	Dark Chocolate Frozen Banana Bites
5	Banana Spinach Muffins	Pork Chops with Balsamic Peppers	Roasted Curried Chickpeas	Pesto Pasta with Ground Turkey	Mango Fruit Leather
6	Fluffy Whole Wheat Zucchini Bread Pancakes	Pan Seared Salmon with Chia Seeds	Easy Roasted Baby Bok Choy	Lemon and Basil Chicken Breasts	Peach & Blueberry Cobbler
7	Whole Wheat Coconut Banana Waffles	Sticky Honey Garlic Chicken Wings	Grain Free Rosemary Crackers	Almond-Crusted Chicken	Carrot Cake

Conclusion

Clean Eating provides your body with a variety of vitamins and minerals, as well as high-quality protein and healthy fats, all of which help to improve heart and brain health, weight management, immune system strength, and energy levels, among other things. Foods that are eaten in their natural state have more flavour.

There are numerous modest, positive methods to improve your nutrition, such as:

- substituting water and herbal tea for soft drinks
- avoiding meat for at least one day a week and ensuring that each meal contains roughly 50% fresh veggies
- consuming whole fruits rather than juices, which have less fibre and often contain added sugar avoiding processed meats, which are high in salt and may raise the risk of colon cancer consuming more lean protein, which can be found in eggs, tofu, fish, and nuts
- taking a cooking lesson and learning how to include more vegetables into meals can also be beneficial

© Copyright 2021 - All rights reserved.

The content contained within this book may not be reproduced, duplicated or transmitted without direct written permission from the author or the publisher.

Under no circumstances will any blame or legal responsibility be held against the publisher, or author, for any damages, reparation, or monetary loss due to the information contained within this book, either directly or indirectly.

Legal Notice:

This book is copyright protected. It is only for personal use. You cannot amend, distribute, sell, use, quote or paraphrase any part, or the content within this book, without the consent of the author or publisher.

Disclaimer Notice:

Please note the information contained within this document is for educational and entertainment purposes only. All effort has been executed to present accurate, up to date, reliable, complete information. No warranties of any kind are declared or implied. Readers acknowledge that the author is not engaged in the rendering of legal, financial, medical or professional advice. The content within this book has been derived from various sources. Please consult a licensed professional before attempting any techniques outlined in this book.

By reading this document, the reader agrees that under no circumstances is the author responsible for any losses, direct or indirect, that are incurred as a result of the use of the information contained within this document, including, but not limited to, errors, omissions, or inaccuracies.

www.ingramcontent.com/pod-product-compliance
Lightning Source LLC
Chambersburg PA
CBHW080608170426

43209CB00007B/1370